THE JOURNALISTS

by the same author

published by Jonathan Cape

THE WESKER TRILOGY
(Chicken Soup with Barley, Roots, I'm Talking About
Jerusalem)

THE KITCHEN

CHIPS WITH EVERYTHING

THE FOUR SEASONS

THEIR VERY OWN AND GOLDEN CITY

THE FRIENDS

FEARS OF FRAGMENTATION

SIX SUNDAYS IN JANUARY

THE OLD ONES

LOVE LETTERS ON BLUE PAPER

SAY GOODBYE, YOU MAY NEVER SEE THEM AGAIN
(paintings by John Allin)

SAID THE OLD MAN TO THE YOUNG MAN

published by The Writers' and Readers' Co-operative

WORDS — AS DEFINITIONS OF EXPERIENCE

FATLIPS

published in 'Plays and Players', April/May 1977

THE WEDDING FEAST

published in 'Adam Magazine', June 1978

THE MERCHANT

Arnold Wesker

THE JOURNALISTS

A Triptych

JONATHAN CAPE
THIRTY BEDFORD SQUARE LONDON

First published 1979
This collection © 1979 by Arnold Wesker
The Journalists © 1975 by Arnold Wesker
'A Journal of *The Journalists*' © 1977 by Arnold Wesker
Journey into Journalism © 1977 by Arnold Wesker

Jonathan Cape Ltd,
30 Bedford Square, London WC1

British Library Cataloguing in Publication Data

Wesker, Arnold
The journalists.
I. Journalism – Great Britain
I. Title II. Wesker, Arnold. Journey into
journalism
822'.9'14   PR6045.E75J/

ISBN 0-224-01444-7

The Journalists was first published in Polish by *Dialog* in
March 1974, and in England by The Writers' and Readers'
Co-operative in 1975. 'A Journal of the Writing of *The
Journalists*' was first published, with the title 'A Journal of
The Journalists', by *Theatre Quarterly*, No. 26, in 1977.
Journey into Journalism was first published by The Writers'
and Readers' Co-operative in 1977.

Performing rights. All performing rights of *The Journalists*
are fully protected, and permission to perform it, whether by
amateurs or professionals, must be obtained in advance from
Robin Dalton, 18 Elm Tree Road, London NW8, who can
furnish all particulars.

Printed in Great Britain by The Anchor Press Ltd
and bound by Wm Brendon & Son Ltd
both of Tiptree, Essex

Contents

Contents

Introduction

The purpose of this brief introduction is simply to establish chronology.

Between June 15th and July 29th, 1971 I sat around the offices of the *Sunday Times* newspaper gathering background information for a play I'd planned to write with a newspaper setting. The notes I made were scribbled in longhand. These were typed on to 40 foolscap sheets. The material for the play was ready but my thoughts about it were unclear.

The idea occurred to me to organise the notes into an extended essay — *Journey into Journalism*. I'd offer it to the *Sunday Times* and even if they couldn't use it I'd have familiarised myself even more intimately with the material of my play. A useful exercise, if nothing else.

On August 31st I began. After two weeks the first draft was done; by November 8th, seven weeks on, the final draft was complete. On that same day I began to write the play and also started the journal of the writing of the play.

Four days later, November 12th, David Jones came to dinner. At that time he was an associate director of the Royal Shakespeare Company with special responsibility for the London season. I told him I was planning a play set in a newspaper office. He became interested. It would have a large cast, I warned. They were looking for plays with a large cast, he said. I asked how long they could wait before finalising their 1972/73 season. January 1972 was given as a deadline.

By November 27th, 1971 the first typed draft was finished. It had taken nineteen days. Another four weeks were spent on the normal process of revising. The second draft was dispatched to David Jones on December 23rd. We both agreed on what further revisions were needed. By the end of July 1972 all rewrites were completed, casting was settled, an opening date – October 29th, 1972 – agreed upon and a contract signed. During June, John Barton offered the roles to the actors in the company. Most of them refused to perform the play and the company abandoned the project. From that time till now the play is the subject of a legal controversy between myself and the Royal Shakespeare Company, and it has received no public professional performance.

Two readings, to raise funds for the Jacksons Lane Community Centre in Highgate, took place at the Centre on Sunday July 13th, 1975. Taking part were many actors from the National Theatre Company and some ex-members of the R.S.C. On March 27th, 1977 an amateur production by the Criterion Theatre took place in Coventry; in 1978 Jugoslav TV made a teleplay, scheduled for transmission in 1979, changing the setting from a newspaper office to a television building; and on June 15th, 1978 French Radio presented a radio version of the play.

Meanwhile *Journey into Journalism* was also going through a set of misfortunes. At first there was great editorial enthusiasm for the work, but a proposal to publish it in the colour supplement was vetoed by higher echelons. I shelved it. Then Jonathan Cape became interested in the piece as a book. I obtained a go-ahead from the editor of the *Sunday Times*, signed a contract and received an advance. But certain journalists on the newspaper objected strongly to its appearance, and after an embattled, sometimes acrimonious correspondence I felt honour-bound to withdraw the essay from publication and return my advance to Cape.

Preface – 1977, on page 189, continues the story.

A.W.

London
September 6th, 1978

THE JOURNALISTS

For Vera Elyashiv —
journalist and dear friend
whose stubbornness helped shape this play.

Introduction

All drama is open to many interpretations. And they are made!

It *is* true that the writer doesn't perceive all the implications of his work, but equally true that the experience he's assembled in the order he's assembled it is intended to be evidence of one or a set of specific explorations.

They may not be the only explorations his work makes—it's in the nature of any assembled evidence that it will suggest the proof of different things to different men, but of all the possible statements a work makes—whether poetically or with a greater degree of prose— one will sound the loudest simply because the author has directed all the selection of his material into making it. One pattern will emerge the strongest because the author has delineated its shape with greater emphasis. What he has taken out in his various drafts he has taken out because he's said: that detracts from my theme, blurs my meaning.

When directors and actors interpret a play they are engaged in the act of discovering that one sound which is louder than the others, that one pattern which is stronger than the others.

Whatever sounds or patterns my audience will find in this work there is only one main one which I intended; may not have achieved but had hoped to.

The Kitchen is not about cooking, it's about man and his relationship to work. *The Journalists* is not about journalism, it's about the poisonous human need to cut better men down to our size, from which need we all suffer in varying degrees. To identify and isolate this need is important because it corrupts such necessary or serious human activities as government, love, revolution or journalism.

Swift wrote a novel which gave this cancerous need a name — Lilliputianism. The lilliputian lover competes with his (or her) loved one instead of complementing her. The lilliputian journalist resents the interviewee's fame, influence or achievement rather than wishing to honour it or caution it or seriously question it. The lilliputian bureaucrat (involved in the same process, but in reverse) seeks to maintain his own size by not acknowledging the possibility of growth in those over whom he officiates; he doesn't *cut* down to size, he *keeps* down to size. The lilliputian revolutionary is more concerned to indulge resentments or pay off private scores than to arrive at real justice.

Thus government, love, revolution or journalism are time and time again betrayed. It is this with which my play is concerned.

London
January 24th, 1975

Production Notes

Is an impressionistic layout of the main offices of the SUNDAY
PAPER. There is a 'cut away' called the CENTRE SPACE where the
action outside the offices is played.

In order that action and dialogue are evenly distributed over
stage area, the designer must pay careful attention as to which
office is near which.

But however the rest is laid out, the NEWS ROOM must
occupy a large space, for most of the final activity goes on there.

To the rear is a screen upon which are projected the huge
printing presses. At a point near the end of the play the projection
is taken over by a film of the presses beginning to roll.

PRODUCTION

Activity must be continuous in all sections throughout the play
while the plot weaves its way stopping here and there – sometimes for a lengthy exchange, sometimes for a few lines. Occasionally conversations will take place on the phone between
individuals from different offices.

While the audience focuses on one 'frame' (section) at a time,
the orchestration of what happens *at the same time* in each
remaining office is a director's problem. The following may help:

The rhythm of a Sunday newspaper office is one of a slow

beginning at the start of the week (Tuesday), working up to an agitated flurry, which culminates at about six in the evening on the Saturday when the button is pushed to start the printing presses rolling for the first editions.

It is important, however, to remember this: it is a Sunday paper, not a daily one; therefore a lot of the pages will be laid out early on in the week. Many articles, indeed, have been set up weeks in advance. This means that not every department is hectic on the Saturday. For example, the Arts Pages are well advanced, but Sport — which is waiting for stories of the Saturday matches — is frantic. The two real centres of Saturday's activity are THE STONE — where the printers and journalists lay out the pages and make the last-minute changes (this area is not shown); and the NEWS ROOM — where the editor and his closest advisers shape up, on blank sheets, the final product. (This area is shown.)

I have not indicated every action, but certain routine movements are continuous throughout — growing in intensity towards the end of the play, and the following actions can be drawn from to help the director in his orchestration:

Messengers taking copy from 'the stone' or from one department to another.

Reporters writing or subs correcting copy at their desks.

Journalists reading newspapers — endlessly! or official documents.

Journalists in conversation in each other's departments.

Journalists shaving themselves with electric razors, women making up (could toilets be shown? They are constantly washing print off their hands).

A woman pushing a tea trolley is ever present; reporters flow to and from it for tea and sandwiches.

Reporters, secretaries at typewriters.

The constant making or receiving of telephone calls.

Individuals with special information being interviewed.

Clatter is continuous but, of course, volume of noise must be regulated or projection of dialogue will be a constant fight for the actors. Could it all be on tape? Then actions could be mimed. I'm thinking particularly of typewriting.

Journalists are alert, fast-thinking and fast-talking individuals. The clue to achieving the right rhythm is to maintain a quick delivery of lines — but in the beginning to have long pauses *between departments* which become shorter as the play continues thus giving the impression of increasing activity.

When action takes place in the CENTRE SPACE the rest of the action and noise freezes.

TIME

This may be a problem since there are many assignments which are concertina'ed. It must be imagined that we are covering a week of five days BUT this week is also five weeks. That is to say, we've taken our Tuesday from the first week, our Wednesday from the second week and so on. Time is therefore taking place on two planes, and some stories belong to the week, others to the five weeks.

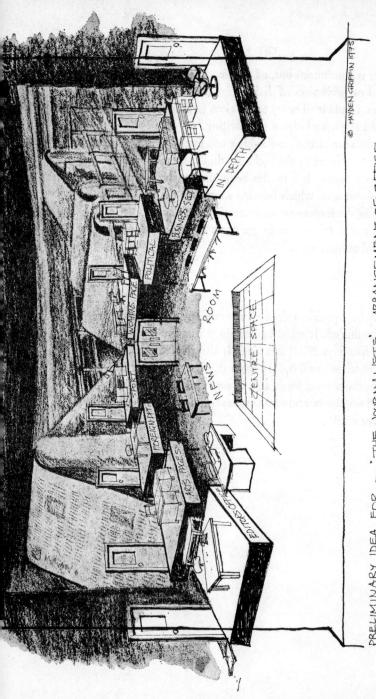

PRELIMINARY IDEA FOR — "THE JOURNALISTS" — ARRANGEMENT OF OFFICE AREAS WITH NEWS ROOM AND INTERVIEW SPACE IN CENTRE THE AREAS BEING USED WOULD BE ISOLATED BY LIGHT ACCESS TO THE AREAS WOULD BE VIA STAIRWAYS BEHIND THE DOORS.

© HAYDEN GRIFFIN 1975

IN DEPTH

BUSINESS SECT

POLITICAL

WOMEN'S PAGE

NEWS ROOM

STORY

FOREIGN DPT.

ARTS PAGES

EDITORS OFFICE

CENTRE SPACE

PRELIMINARY IDEA FOR: "THE JOURNALISTS" — USE OF A SMALL ROSTRUM TRUCKED ON "THROUGH CENTRE BACK" OR BROUGHT UP ON STAGE LEFT FORMING "INTERVIEW AREA"

© HAYDEN GRIFFIN 1975

Characters

MARY MORTIMER   A 'columnist'

HARVEY WINTERS   The editor

CHRIS MACKINTOSH   Journalists on In Depth
JULIAN GALAGHER

PAUL MANNERING   News editor

HARRY LAURISTON   News reporters
MARTIN CRUIKSHANK

ANTHONY SHARPLES   Business News editor

MORTY COHEN   Business News journalists
DOMINIC FLETCHER

JANE MERRYWEATHER   Women's Pages journalists
ANGELA GOURNEY

SEBASTIAN HERBERT   Arts Pages editor
JOHN PROSSER   Assistant Arts Pages editor
ERNST GUEST   A novelist, reviewer

RONNIE SHAPIRO   Sports editor

MARVIN MCKEVIN   Assistant Sports editor

GORDON FAIRCHILD   Foreign editor
TAMARA DRAZIN   A foreign correspondent

NORMAN HARDCASTLE   Journalists working in
CYNTHIA TREVELYAN   Political and Features

SECRETARY	to the editor
SECRETARY	in the News Room
PAT STERLING	A freelance journalist
SIR ROLAND SHAWCROSS	Minister of State for Social Services
RT HON. GEORGE CARRON	Minister of State for Science and Technology
SIR REGINALD MACINTYRE	Chancellor of the Exchequer
OLIVER MASSINGHAM	Under-Secretary of State for Foreign and Commonwealth Affairs
A FINK	A man with 'secret' information
AGNES	Daughter and sons of
JONATHAN	Mary Mortimer
DESMOND	
MAC SMITH	A trade union official — Municipal and Gen.

Thirty-three characters in all, excluding
MESSENGERS, SUBS, REPORTERS

Set designs suggested by HAYDEN GRIFFIN

The cast in the rehearsed readings in the Jacksons Lane Community Centre were:

Mary Mortimer	SHEILA ALLEN
Harvey Winters	IAN MCKELLEN
Chris Mackintosh	SEBASTIAN GRAHAM JONES
Julian Galagher	WILLIAM HOYLAND
Paul Mannering	MICHAEL MELLINGER
Harry Lauriston	DAVE HILL
Martin Cruikshank	DAVID BRADLEY
Anthony Sharples	GAWN GRAINGER
Morty Cohen	OLIVER COTTON
Dominic Fletcher	JOHN HUG
Jane Merryweather	KATHERINE FAHY
Angela Gourney	JANET KEY
Sebastian Herbert	BERNARD GALLAGHER
John Prosser	HUGH THOMAS
Ernst Guest	BRIAN BADCOE
Ronnie Shapiro	HARRY LANDIS
Marvin McKevin	JIM NORTON
Gordon Fairchild	JOHN BENNETT
Tamara Drazin	LISA HARROW
Norman Hardcastle	BRIAN COX
Cynthia Trevelyan	GILLIAN BARGE

Secretary	LIZ HUGHES
Pat Sterling	JENNIE STOLLER
Sir Rowland Shawcross	ROBERT EDDISON
Rt Hon. George Carron	MARK DIGNAM
Sir Reginald Macintyre	PETER JEFFREY
Oliver Massingham	JOHN GILL
A Fink	JONATHAN PRYCE
Agnes	CHERYL CAMPBELL
Jonathan	DAVID YELLAND
Desmond	ANDREW BYATT
Mac Smith	FULTON MACKAY
Messengers, Subs, Reporters	LINDSAY JOE WESKER
	ARNOLD WESKER

Directed by	MICHAEL KUSTOW
Designed and lit by	HAYDEN GRIFFIN
	RORY DEMPSTER
Casting by	GILLIAN DIAMOND
Assistant to the Director	JULIA WEEKS

ACT I

PART ONE

THE CENTRE SPACE

MARY MORTIMER *is interviewing* SIR ROLAND SHAWCROSS, *Minister for Social Services, in his office. There's a tape-recorder on the desk.*

SHAWCROSS. And that, Miss Mortimer, is precisely what democracy is: a risky balancing act. The delicate arrangement of laws in a way that enables the state to conduct its affairs freely without impinging upon the reasonable freedom of the individual. Tilt it too much one way or the other and either side, state or individual, seizes up, unable to act to its fullest capacity.

MARY. But surely, Minister, with respect, and I know you've written standard textbooks on the subject, you must agree that the *quality* of democracy doesn't *only* depend on the balance of freedom which our laws create between the individual and society, does it?

SHAWCROSS. By which you mean?

MARY. By which I mean that ordinary men are forced, daily, to confront the depressing petty officials who interpret those laws.

SHAWCROSS. Therefore?

MARY. Therefore *you* may give the letter to the law but the spirit of the law filters through to the ordinary citizen in the waiting rooms of hospitals, the offices of the employment exchange, the desks of housing officials, visits of social security officers and –

SHAWCROSS. Go on.

MARY. I could go on endlessly, Sir Roland.

SHAWCROSS. Go on endlessly. I don't see your question yet.

MARY. Well, I'm rather intimidated about going on, you've said these things much better than ever I could.

SHAWCROSS. Be brave.

MARY. Alright. Great wisdom and learning may be required to *conceive* statutes but who expects great wisdom and learning in officials? And the ordinary man meets *them* not *you*. He faces the policeman, the factory superintendent, the tax-collector, the traffic warden — in fact the whole gamut of middle men whose officious behaviour affects the temper and pleasure of everyday life.

SHAWCROSS. And your question is?

MARY. What concern do you have for that?

SHAWCROSS. For the gap between the law maker and the law receiver?

MARY. No, with respect, I'd put it another way. For the change in the *quality* of the law which takes place when mediocre men are left to interpret it.

SHAWCROSS. That sounds like a very arrogant view of your fellow creatures, Miss Mortimer.

MARY. Sir Roland, forgive me, I must say it, but that's evasive. (*Intercom buzzer rings.*)

VOICE. Your car in fifteen minutes, Minister.

SHAWCROSS. Thank you. (*Pause*) Miss Mortimer, our first hour is nearly up. Tomorrow you're dining with us at home — it is tomorrow, I think? We can continue then. But for the moment I'd like to speak off the record. You've created a very unique reputation in journalism. Rightly and properly you're investigating the minds and personalities of men who shape policy. And you're doing it in depth, in our offices, our homes and on social occasions. I'm surprised so many of us have agreed and perhaps it will prove a mistake. We'll see. But there are aspects of government which it's obviously foolish of us to discuss in public no matter how eager we are to be seen being open and frank. You want me to say what concern I have for the actual quality of everyman's daily life. I could answer simply, and honestly, *every* concern. But where does that get us? I could project myself as an all-round humanitarian but — I know I'd not be called upon to demonstrate that humanity. I could offer you phrases which my own, canny experience tells me will look good in print. But you're after something different and I, for one, would like to help you find something different. I'm not evasive but, to be blunt, some of my harshest thoughts could be demoralising. Ah! you will say, that is the part of the man I'm after. But consider this: how true is the truth? You're right, the ordinary man must face the numb and bureaucratic mind. Our best intentions are distorted by such minds. But that can't really be my area of concern, can it? Suppose it were, I might then be forced to observe that the petty mind is a product of a petty education. Should I then go to complain to the Minister of Education? He might then say education is only *part* of the influence on a growing person — there's family environment to be considered. Should he then interfere in everyman's home? No, no, no! Only God knows where wisdom comes from, you can't legislate for it. Government can only legislate for the *common* good; the *individual* good is, I'm afraid, what men must iron out among themselves. Now, that's the 'truth' about my thinking. But how 'true' is it? I don't act on it. My attempts at legislation are not less excellent because I doubt the excellence of men to interpret them. So, which truth will you tell? You have three: that I aspire to perfection of the law? That I mistrust the middle men who must exercise that law? Or will you combine the two? The first is pompous, the second abusive, the third confusing.

MARY. And you don't think people would respond to such honesty?

SHAWCROSS. No! Frankly. Most people can't cope with honesty.

MARY. With respect, Minister, but that sounds like a very arrogant view of your fellow creatures.

SHAWCROSS. Ha! (*Pause*) We'll continue, we'll continue. I must leave.

(*Both go to door which he holds open.*)

And it's not necessary to keep saying 'with respect', Miss Mortimer. Do you enjoy saying it? Funny thing, but people enjoy saying things like 'your honour', 'your Majesty', 'with respect', 'your highness' ...

Now the offices of the SUNDAY PAPER burst into activity.

EDITOR'S OFFICE

HARVEY WINTERS, *the editor, dictating to secretary.*

HARVEY. ' ... And so, you ask, "Where do the best minds go? Not into politics or the civil service," you say, "there's no role for this country to perform—instead they go into journalism and the mass media." Well, I don't agree with your parenthetical observation but it's a good question and a flattering answer. The best minds don't want to legislate or exercise power, so they comment! Journalism as an act of creating self-awareness in society! Good! And for that very reason I believe it matters intensely the way newspapers,

radio and television report race relations. Spectacularly in
India, the Ahmedabad, A-H-M-E-D-A-B-A-D, the Ahmedabad riot was touched off by rumours given the apparent
veracity of print: stealthily in Britain, the malformed seeds of
prejudice have been watered by a rain of false statistics and
stories. Television news has been an offender—no, a *gross*
offender; the interviewer asks people in the street what they
think and the weirdest notions of reality are listened to with
the respect accorded to truth, as if the electronic marvel of it
all sanctified the instant communication of ignorance.' *(Phone
rings.)* Bloody hell! I'll never finish those letters. No calls after
this. Hello, Winters.

(It's ANTHONY SHARPLES, *editor of Business News.*

ANTHONY. You rang.

HARVEY. Tony, yes. I want you to do something on women
being allowed into the Stock Exchange.

ANTHONY. Love to. Can't claim the privileges of a private club,
now, can they?

HARVEY. I was thinking of a light-hearted leader, not an
occasion for solemnity.

ANTHONY. Indeed not, no, indeed. They've made fools enough
of themselves. Now let's see if they're still worried about
telling dirty jokes on the floor. How many words.

HARVEY. About 450?

ANTHONY. Done.

IN DEPTH

Two journalists: CHRIS MACKINTOSH, JULIAN GALAGHER.

CHRIS *(tearing sheet from pad)*. Falling bloody bridges! This subject must have priority over something, though God knows what.

JULIAN (*banging on phone receiver*). Hello? Hello? Blast! Going through to someone else. (*To* CHRIS) Here's that couple of quid I owe you.

BUSINESS NEWS

This is a large section only part of which we see, the rest tails off-stage. Three journalists: ANTHONY SHARPLES, MORTY COHEN, DOMINIC FLETCHER.

DOMINIC (*who's been listening on a phone, shouts, off-stage*). There's a stringer here says that the Transport and General Workers' Union in the north have an eccentric official who's bored with head office contracts. He insists that every new contract *he* draws up has to have an original clause in it and this time he's insisted that every man gets a day off on his birthday. Anybody interested?

VOICE (*off-stage*). Try Features.

DOMINIC (*into phone*). An incredibly stupid suggestion from one of my colleagues to try Features.

IN DEPTH

CHRIS. *I* don't know why the bloody bridges fall down. I don't even know why they keep up.

JULIAN (*pointing to pile of documents while hanging on to a phone*). By the time we read through this lot we'll be able to build them ourselves. Hello hello HELLO!

CHRIS. Have you got hold of anyone yet?

JULIAN. Going through to someone else now. Hello? Press office? At last. It took five people to get to you. Julian Galagher, the *Sunday Paper*, here. These bridges that keep falling down. Is your ministry making a statement yet?

EDITOR'S OFFICE

MARY *knocks and enters.*

SECRETARY. Good God! How triumphant she looks.

MARY. They're going to work.

HARVEY. What was he like?

MARY. Shrewd, evasive and charmingly civilised.

SECRETARY. She's obviously enjoying herself.

MARY. Loving it.

SECRETARY. Why, Mary Mortimer, you're even radiant.

MARY. Don't I deserve to be? I worked bloody hard to set up those interviews and they're all going to happen.

HARVEY. We all worked hard—

SECRETARY. —had to pull strings you know.

HARVEY. The notorious side of your brilliance isn't the most helpful key for opening the doors of power.

MARY. You've got the best journalist on Fleet Street working for you, stop complaining.

HARVEY. You'll not expect me to do that.

MARY. Quite right, Harvey.

SECRETARY. So you'd better lose that smug radiance before it tempts ...

MARY. ... my sardonic colleagues to demolish me with their courteous male chauvinism.

HARVEY. You getting your ministers to talk on the science-versus-politics issue?

MARY. I'm free-ranging over everything.

HARVEY. Because I want us to build up a body of comment on that issue and your profiles will be central. I'm planning TV trailers on them the second you finish the last interview.

MARY. It's not easy. Not everyone sees the future as you do in terms of science versus politics.

HARVEY. We'll help them then.

MARY. And I trust you're planning to plaster the Saturday screen with the maximum spots?

HARVEY. Don't teach your granny to suck eggs.

MARY. Even granny's male pride is a little punctured, isn't it?

HARVEY. And don't draw me into one of your sex wars, love.

MARY. Confess. Liberated though you may be, Harvey Winters, women do not a paper make. Confess.

HARVEY. I'm not biting. Now be a good girl and go. Look! Letters!

MARY. I'm going. Got me laundry spinning round the corner.

WOMEN'S PAGES

Two journalists: JANE MERRYWEATHER, ANGELA GOURNEY.

JANE *(just entering with mocked-up sheets)*. Not a very inspiring week's work, is it? An article about women's bums, one about two awful designers who make men's suits for £150 each and another about wild tea-drinking parties.

ANGELA. We're only supposed to be able to write about boys and knickers. Stop complaining.

IN DEPTH

CHRIS. Do I want a cigarette? Yes, I do want a cigarette. *(Reaching for packet.)* No, I don't want a cigarette. Bridges! Christ! What a come-down for In Depth.

POLITICAL AND FEATURES

Two journalists: NORMAN HARDCASTLE, CYNTHIA TREVELYAN.

CYNTHIA. Look at these photographs. We've created a monster.
NORMAN. Aargh! The maimed, the dead, the diseased —
CYNTHIA. — and the starving. Look at them.
NORMAN. Someone must do them but I don't want to look at them.
CYNTHIA. And I can't get him to snap anything else now. 'Where the violence is, send me there,' he says. And he's right. He can't photograph peace. And it's our fault. We've encouraged a morbid squint in his eye. My fault in fact. Bloody hell! They make me feel so wretched.

EDITOR'S OFFICE

HARVEY. What's on today?
SECRETARY. You mustn't forget to speak to Chris Mackintosh about the collapse of Atlantis Insurance.
HARVEY. After the eleven o'clock.

SECRETARY. After the eleven o'clock. Then lunch with Morgan King, M.P.

HARVEY. The new fiery socialist superstar.

SECRETARY. The very same. Then the boss wants you at five.

HARVEY. Can't see myself in a fit state for him after three hours of wine and fiery socialism.

POLITICAL AND FEATURES

CYNTHIA. When he first came here he could hardly talk. Just threw his photographs on the desk and asked could we use them. In those days I pretended ugliness had poetry. Blocks of new flats with graffiti on the lift doors, smouldering kids hanging around the stairs, fighting on the roundabouts. Even then he had an eye for violence and desolation and waste. His own background. Look at them. Not even pity, is there? Just acceptance. 'This is how it is!' And every time he comes in with a new batch of evidence about cruelty it shows in his own features.

NEWS ROOM

A SECRETARY, *who spends most of her time answering the phone, taking down messages and handing them to the news editor,* PAUL MANNERING.

Two reporters: HARRY LAURISTON, MARTIN CRUIKSHANK.

MARTIN *(waving newspaper)*. Another cutting to give to the honourable Miss Mary Mortimer for her Morgan King, M.P., file.

HARRY. Where's he been speaking this time?

MARTIN. Humbermouth. Quote: 'Opening the town hall in the latest new town of Humbermouth, Mr Morgan King, the socialist M.P. for New Lannark, upset councillors by attacking what he called "the dead spirit of the place". In a speech which can't have endeared him to the town's architects he said: "But where is your town's spirit? This town hall? A building where functionaries meet to organise your tax and drainage problems? Surely," the fiery M.P. for New Lannark continued, "a town's heart is its gardens, its concert hall, its swimming pool, libraries, meeting places — where are they?"'

PAUL. Splendid. I've no doubt the bitch'll go to town on that one.

POLITICAL AND FEATURES

NORMAN. Jesus! I've got a lump in my throat.

CYNTHIA. Give up smoking.

NORMAN. It's all right for you to be flippant.

CYNTHIA. Who's flippant? You got a lump in your throat, so stop smoking.

NORMAN. You also think it might be cancer?

CYNTHIA. Norman, for God's sake.

BUSINESS NEWS

DOMINIC. So I charms into me lap the lovely tennis player, who's also rich, privileged and American, and says to her,

'Ho hum, you think that now you're in my arms I'll not put out that story?' 'But,' she says, 'I thought you were a business journalist not a sports reporter.' 'I am, I am,' says I, 'but,' I pretend to her, 'the lesbian love affair of a famous Wimbledon player is too good for any kind of journalist to let slip.' With which she jumps out from the comfort of my ample thighs and cries, 'It's a terrible profession, terrible! Have you no standards?' 'Standards?' I say. 'Profession?' I say. 'I don't believe journalists have a profession – I don't know what that profession is anyway. And certainly they don't have any standards. It's the law of the jungle!' I cry. 'And not a very colourful one at that!' But, soft Irish nit that I am, I relent and in the end swop my silence for a night in the net – in a manner of speaking.

EDITOR'S OFFICE

NORMAN *visiting*.

NORMAN. How about letting me take a look at the guerrillas in East Pakistan?

HARVEY. Climate's rotten. You know you catch whatever disease is in the air.

NORMAN. I'm serious, Harvey.

HARVEY. So am I.

NORMAN. You haven't got a better person in this paper to do it.

HARVEY. Bloody hell! The egos in this building.

WOMEN'S PAGES

ANGELA. We're not used enough. We ought to be more pro-vocative instead of practical. 'Down with children' not 'Cheap canvas chairs from Chelsea'. 'Down with children'. 'Must mothers of handicapped children be martyrs?' That sort of thing. Dammit! We're paid well enough. I want to be stretched. *(With its double entendre)* I luuuuve being stretched.

EDITOR'S OFFICE

HARVEY *(on the phone to* CYNTHIA*)*. Cynthia, is Norman near by?
CYNTHIA. No.
HARVEY. He having problems with his wife?
CYNTHIA. Afraid so. Why?
HARVEY. He's pressing me about going abroad again.
CYNTHIA. Guerrillas in East Pakistan?
HARVEY. The same. What's his illness this week?
CYNTHIA. Cancer of the throat.
HARVEY. Bloody hell! I'll talk to Gordon.

ARTS PAGES

SEBASTIAN HERBERT, *Arts Pages editor;* JOHN PROSSER, *assistant;* ERNST GUEST, *a novelist and reviewer.*

JOHN. It's 9,000. I've finished counting. Last year we received

9,000 books to review, of which we succeeded in covering roughly one fifth — nearly 2,000 in fact.

ERNST. Is that good or bad?

SEBASTIAN. Very good, my boy. What, 1,900 books in 52 weeks? Work it out.

ERNST. You work it out.

SEBASTIAN. I will, I will. That's let's see, 52 into 340, six — that's roughly 36 books a week which, although many are reviews in brief, is pretty good going. *And* you must take into account that with declining advertising the paper's not as big as it can be most of the time. Yes, very good I'd say.

EDITOR'S OFFICE

GORDON FAIRCHILD *of Foreign dept. visiting.*

HARVEY. I'd like the research to begin now, Gordon. Go right back to the Aryan invasions of India, who was Hinduised, which minorities remained, the role of Imperial England in protecting minorities, why did the Muslims survive, right up to partition of Pakistan from India.

GORDON. What about the power of the priests?

HARVEY. Right! You can give a break-down on the sects as well.

GORDON. I'm thinking of something more on the lines of linking the massacres to the religious rabble-rousers.

HARVEY. Too big. It's a separate piece.

GORDON. But central, don't you think?

HARVEY. I know that priests everywhere have a lot to answer for and one day we'll write it — something for Tamara perhaps — but not now. This massacre's enough. O.K.?

GORDON. As you say.

SPORTS PAGES

RONNIE SHAPIRO, *Sports editor*. MARVIN MCKEVIN, *his assistant*.

RONNIE. Fascist! That's what it is. All sport is fascist activity. I've just realised.

MARVIN. Only just?

RONNIE. Governed by rules against which there's no appeal.

MARVIN. You've been talking to too many referees.

RONNIE. I mean apply them to a democratic society and they wouldn't hold up for ten seconds.

MARVIN. How about taking over the Arts Pages for six months?

RONNIE. And what's more fascist than all that crap about healthy body healthy mind?

MARVIN. And character being built on the playing fields of Eton?

RONNIE. All balls. *What* character, that's the point. The Arts Pages? I'd love to.

FOREIGN DEPT.

TAMARA DRAZIN, *foreign correspondent*. GORDON, *just entering*.

GORDON. Harvey wants us to keep going at Pakistan.

TAMARA *(with irony)*. He's not afraid of 'boring' our readers?

GORDON. Even if it does.

TAMARA. Small blessings.

GORDON. And I agree with him.

TAMARA. And I'm sick. Look at it. *(Indicating telex reports.)* For what? What in this world is worth such savage slaughter?

GORDON. Keep cuts to a minimum then.

TAMARA. Cut it? I want to weep on it.

ARTS PAGES

ERNST. I can't understand why you don't raise the price of newspapers.

JOHN. Cut down our dependence on advertising? No point really. Newspapers are a dying institution.

SEBASTIAN. Needless to say, I don't share that view.

JOHN. Get in all the reviews you can, Ernst my boy. The day of the newspaper mogul is over. We're the honoured custodians of his agonising death cries. He's screwed everyone, made off with his millions and now the workers are screwing back and between them they'll soon end an era. What you're witnessing is the decline of an industry.

FOREIGN DEPT.

TAMARA *is cutting out her clippings and pasting them in her book.*

TAMARA. Look how full my book's getting.

GORDON. I've an idea which I put to Harvey and he likes.

TAMARA. Do you know why we all keep scrap books of our little bits and pieces?

GORDON. It's a serious long-term project for you, listen to me.

TAMARA. So that in twenty years' time we can say, 'Look! *I* was right. When everyone else was making the wrong analysis of a situation I was making the right one. Here it is. In print!'

GORDON. An in-depth probe into the power of the priests.

TAMARA. Even Harvey.

GORDON. The priests have a lot to answer for, you know.

TAMARA. Even Harvey will point to a passage in a new bill and say, 'Look! My wording! Exactly what I wrote in an editorial a hundred years ago.'

GORDON. Something on the lines of linking massacres to the religious rabble-rousers.

TAMARA. 'They've listened to me,' we all cry.

GORDON. And, for God's sake, listen to *me*.

TAMARA. What priests? There are priests and priests.

GORDON. All dogma begins with the priesthood. And where there's dogma there's massacre.

TAMARA. I'm not fit, Gordon, believe me, I'm not fit.

NEWS ROOM

PAT STERLING, *a freelance, talking to* PAUL.

PAUL. I don't think it's our story, Pat, not really. Aren't girls of twelve having abortions all the time?

PAT. But this one had been refused by a National Health Service gynaecologist. Some shrivelled-up hag.

PAUL. We can't help being shrivelled-up old hags, you know, and isn't it all over anyhow?

PAT. That's why you can print the story.

PAUL. And the poor child's had her abortion privately?

PAT. 'If you play adult games,' says this gynaecologist, 'you must expect adult consequences.'

PAUL. Awful, yes, I know, terrible story. Have you tried the *News of the World*?

PAT. Don't you just *know* what they'd do with it?

SECRETARY. The eleven o'clock in five minutes, Paul.

PAUL *(assembling papers)*. I'm sorry.

FOREIGN DEPT.

GORDON. Perhaps you should see a psychiatrist.

TAMARA. Uch! They're so immodest.

GORDON. I know a good one.

TAMARA. They imagine every distress is a curable aberration.

GORDON. Did you know I was under one for three years?

TAMARA. Think they can explain everything. 'The fault of the past! A sad tangle of human relationships!' Such awful presumptions. I despise them.

GORDON. Why don't you ever listen to me?

TAMARA. And you know why I despise them? Because there's such a thing as *endemic* despair only they're too arrogant to acknowledge it; you can't *pay* to have *that* cut out.

GORDON. Friends can help.

TAMARA. Maybe. But not help to get rid of it, only to live with it. Endemic despair is something you're born with.

GORDON. Or something you have if you can afford it.

TAMARA. That's a vulgar observation.

GORDON. You mean it's vulgar to be so poor that you've no time to reflect upon endemic despairs?

TAMARA. No, but it's crude to observe it.

GORDON. *Crude* to observe it? You've changed your mind? No longer 'vulgar'?

TAMARA. Don't split hairs.

GORDON. Well now, let's take a look at that, then. Crude to observe that the starving child has no time to reflect on life's hopelessness?

TAMARA. Ah ha! The starving child. He had to be brought in.

GORDON. Don't sneer at the starving child, my dear. Without him you'd have no endemic despair to enjoy.

TAMARA. You think I enjoy despair? You're a demagogue, Gordon.

GORDON. Scorn not the man who doth attempt alleviation of man's ills.

TAMARA. Scorn such a man I do not. But man's relentless and ugly stupidities are mine to despair of. You want to do good deeds? Do them. I will give you my cheque and God bless you. But do them silently and not heartily and give me leave to lament what I will.

GORDON. I'm even more convinced you need help.

TAMARA. And don't insult me.

(*She leaves.* MARTIN *passes her, extending a greeting she ignores.*)

MARTIN. She's getting worse.

GORDON. She worries me. She's speaking louder, faster and, with her deep-throated Slavic accent, she's becoming like a Noël Coward caricature.

MARTIN. A man just rang in, American, freelance. Says he's got a trunkload of documents that reveals the 'truth about Biafra'!

GORDON. That'll make the fourth trunkload of documents I'll have read revealing the 'truth about Biafra'.

MARTIN (*imitating*). 'Oh boy, man, is this big. Wait till you get a load of this. *This* is really big.'

GORDON. They're all big.

SPORTS PAGES

MARVIN *entering.*

MARVIN. Bloody hell!

RONNIE. I'm not interested.

MARVIN. Those phoney sports stories in the *Daily Sun* I've been blasting?

RONNIE. What of them?

MARVIN. Harvey stopped me this morning and said lay off.

RONNIE. *That* he should've said to me.

MARVIN. 'Lay off,' he said, 'my opposite number is squealing.'

RONNIE. Are we trying to change sports reporting or are we not trying to change sports reporting!?

> *(Phone rings. It's* HARVEY *from the editor's office.)*

HARVEY. Ronnie?

RONNIE. Yes, Harvey.

HARVEY. Yesterday's *Financial Times.* Page 12. Second column, three up from the bottom. Got it?

RONNIE *(who's been turning pages of the* F.T.*).* Got it.

HARVEY. Aston Vale football club is offering you, me and others shareholdings in the club. Might make a good story for 'Bullseye'. Who's selling them, how many, why, and who's buying. O.K.?

RONNIE. O.K. Thanks. *(Phone down)*

EDITOR'S OFFICE

It has been slowly filling up with people for the eleven o'clock editorial meeting.

Present are ANTHONY SHARPLES, CHRIS MACKINTOSH, GORDON FAIRCHILD.

HARVEY *(to* ANTHONY, *and having just put down the phone).* You going to stop reading that paper and listen to us?

ANTHONY. When *you've* stopped phoning.

HARVEY. Right, gentlemen. And what are we going to do about our beloved leader and his government this week?

GORDON. I think it's about time we tried a touch of irony in our political commentaries. 'Today poverty is your own fault, today you can stand on your own two feet. Anyone can become Prime Minister.'

CHRIS. 'Our beloved leader has proved it.'

GORDON. 'And our nasty chancellor has proved it. All of them self-made and nasty men saying you too can also all be self-made and nasty men …'

CHRIS. Think they'll get the point? *(To* GORDON*)* Here's that couple of quid I owe you.

POLITICAL AND FEATURES

TAMARA *visiting.*

CYNTHIA. 'Why so pale and wan, fond lover?'

TAMARA. I think what I'd like is a good, old-fashioned nervous breakdown.

CYNTHIA. That's a shocking thing to say, Tamara.

TAMARA. There's such honesty about going to pieces.

CYNTHIA. You mustn't be frivolous about such things.

TAMARA. I feel so guilty to find myself being able to cope with it all.

NORMAN. Guilts! Guilts! Those sombre, Jewish guilts.

TAMARA. Mornings. Wake up. A disc jockey's forced jocularity.

CYNTHIA. Well, thank God for a little jocularity, I say.

TAMARA. These offices. Sour jealousies. Battles for space. Defeated journalists.

NORMAN. *Not* first day of the week, pleeease.

TAMARA *(picking up newspaper and turning pages)*. Then all this. The smug weariness of experienced politicians. The intimidations of bigoted minorities. The tortuous self-defence of money makers. The pomposity of knowledge-glutted academics. Genocide in Pakistan. And us, pretending to stand up to them with I-don't-know-what; our 500 words here, our 600-word thoughts there.

NORMAN. The price we pay for the pleasure of your company is the depressing effects of your conversation.

ARTS PAGES

ERNST *(who is checking his proofs)*. Sebastian, is it your idea of a joke, a correction, or an improvement to change the words of my review from 'to put it mildly' to 'to put it wildly'?

SEBASTIAN. Oh, here's a much better printer's error. *(Reading from a proof.)* 'They become incredibly wound up; yet these is method in their madness for the unwinding is ceremonies and without a bitch.'

POLITICAL AND FEATURES

CYNTHIA. As a matter of fact, I'm about to embark on a long eulogy of disc jockeys.

TAMARA. Really.

CYNTHIA. All about the joy they bring to drab lives.

TAMARA. And how their constant stream of gaiety denies the existence of unhappiness?

CYNTHIA. Not denies, just bypasses.

TAMARA. There's nothing more gloomy than laughter at all costs.

CYNTHIA. It's not laughter at all costs, it's music at all costs.

TAMARA. *Music?*

CYNTHIA. Yes! Yes! Music!

TAMARA. No! No! *Not* music. Energy, perhaps, of a spurious urgency, and a relentless loudness to cover up for poverty of talent.

CYNTHIA. You're growing old and square.

TAMARA. What an easy vocabulary of insults we have these days. 'Square' presumably is the state you need to think others are in so that you can feel young? *(She leaves.)*

CYNTHIA. How complicated these mid-European ladies are.

EDITOR'S OFFICE

Editorial continuing.
PAUL *from News Desk entering.*

HARVEY. Hello, Paul. Our problem is that we're all in agreement that government's wrong and we're right.

ANTHONY. Oh, I don't know. I'm more inflationary than you.

HARVEY. Are you? Well, you're wrong then. I think we're entitled to be absolutely critical of *all* aspects by now and it would be absolutely consistent with our policy to criticise the government's economic strategy.

ANTHONY. There *is* no economic strategy.

GORDON. But there *is* a philosophy. I mean 'let lame ducks go to the wall and stand on your own two feet' *is* a philosophy.

ANTHONY. Yes, but it's not a strategy.

HARVEY. Anyway, they're changing doctrines. State subsidy, for industries suffering from 'non-culpable decline'.

ANTHONY. From what?

HARVEY. 'Intervention in industry,' says the minister in today's *Times*, 'is respectable in areas of non-culpable decline.' What do we say to that?

GORDON. Sounds like a very sad and touching excuse for death. 'Please, everyone, forgive my non-culpable decline.'

BUSINESS NEWS

MORTY. The great thing about Arnold Weinstock is — the man's so sane.

DOMINIC. What is there about shopkeepers, d'you think, that mesmerises the intelligent journalists of Business News?

MORTY. If he has to sack 5,000 men because of waste he'll do it. And he'll justify it by saying it's better for the sacked ones because men get depressed hanging around doing nothing, lose self-respect.

DOMINIC. Compassionate man, Weinstock.

MORTY. And those that stay know that they're good because Weinstock has kept them and so they're men of confidence.

DOMINIC. A Solomon, no less!

MORTY. His prime task? To weed out a waste.

DOMINIC. A gardener, to boot!

MORTY. He appeals to men's greed but, paradoxically —

DOMINIC. — paradoxically —

MORTY. — paradoxically he must elicit from them a high degree of *co-operation* in order to satisfy that greed.

DOMINIC. Paradoxically.

MORTY. His approach is precisely that of a good business journalist — determined to cut through half-truths and vague generalisations.

DOMINIC. Really?

MORTY. 'Never believe anything,' he says, 'all information is suspect.'

DOMINIC. Arnold Weinstock's attitude is rather like that of the baron of whom it was asked: 'Why do you build your walls so high and strong?' To which the baron replied: 'In order to give the peasants' hovels something to lean upon.'

EDITOR'S OFFICE

Editorial continuing.

HARVEY. Where are we on the Soviet spaceship deaths?

PAUL. No further than any other newspaper.

GORDON. Anyone know why the monkey died last time?

ANTHONY. Boredom, I think.

POLITICAL AND FEATURES

MARY *rushes in with her bag of laundry.*

MARY. I'm late for the eleven o'clock.

NORMAN. We've got another Morgan King quote for you. Cynthia?

CYNTHIA *(reading from a cutting).* 'Addressing the annual Durham
    Miners' gala over the weekend, Mr Morgan King, the new
    fiery socialist superstar member for New Lannark, said: "I
    believe that before any legislation can be passed in parliament
    there must exist the machinery to communicate an under-
    standing of that legislation, otherwise we will be forced to
    drag a community behind us." '

MARY. What the bloody hell does he think newspapers and
    television are for?

CYNTHIA. ' "Nor is it enough to print, however vast the quantity,
    our complex blue bills and white papers which few can read
    or understand, nor to leave their interpretation to the not-
    always-adequately-briefed and random intelligence of busy,
    information-drunk journalists who interpret according to
    bias or the quality of their mind." '

MARY. The impertinence! The incredible impertinence of the
    man. How dare he? 'The quality of their mind'. Who the
    bloody hell does he think he is. A jumped-up miner's son
    with exaggerated notions about the value of self-education!

NORMAN. Uh-uh-uh-uh!

MARY. Well, *I'm* not intimidated by working-class haloes – the
    pain of poverty has never blinded me to its product of ignor-
    ance, and underprivilege was never a guarantee against
    charlatanism and *that's* the function of journalism – to protect
    society from shabby little charlatans like him.

NORMAN. And who will protect society from shabby little
    journalists? We traffic in human blemishes, Mary. Don't you
    find it washing over your own life?

MARY. I'll take you on some other time. *(Rushes out.)*

WOMEN'S PAGES

JANE. Do you know what Mary said to me when I first came to work here? 'If you're young and in charge,' she said, 'and you want to deflate an old journalist, my advice to you is this: when she — or he — brings his piece to you, you flip through it and then throw it on the desk and say, "Well, honestly, I didn't expect you to show me something like this." '

ANGELA. That sounds like our Mary. What made you think of that?

JANE. Don't know. Remember the time we invited the politicos to our ideas luncheon and we ended up giving *them* ideas? Well, I gave the idea for those in-depth interviews of cabinet ministers to Norman and — well — oh, I don't know. Credit grabbing is one of the sicknesses of this profession. Takes it out of you.

IN DEPTH

NORMAN *visiting*.

NORMAN. Where's your master?

JULIAN. Don't have masters or deputies in our department. Some of us just get paid more than others, that's all.

NORMAN. Worthy, worthy.

JULIAN. Being someone's deputy is an invitation to assassination. He knows it, I know it, so we drop titles. Lovely life. Easy, civilised, just what I was born to. Scurrying across Europe to investigate this and that, pause for a love affair, a ballet, a bit of skiing. You ever go skiing, Norman?

NORMAN. Are you mad? Skiing? You can break legs and die of exposure and things.

JULIAN. Glad to see you making jokes about your dying and disease. Good to laugh at one's fears, I think.

NORMAN. I'm not laughing. That's the mistake everyone makes. *I* ceased laughing after Molière. Humour for me is an internal haemorrhage, otherwise it's contrived giggles.

EDITOR'S OFFICE

Editorial continuing.
MARY *entering.*

HARVEY. Hello, Mary. I think we ought to have someone in India in case war breaks out.

ANTHONY. In *case* war breaks out? With six million East Pakistani refugees on her soil and every major power full of pious platitudes? War? *And* revolution, *and* famine, *and* cholera.

HARVEY. Any volunteers to go?

GORDON. Me please.

HARVEY. You'll bloody stay here and co-ordinate.

ANTHONY. No free trips this time, my lad.

HARVEY. I'm thinking of sending Norman to take a look at the Mukti Bahani.

GORDON. You thinking or is he asking?

SPORTS PAGES

MAC SMITH, *a trade union official, visiting.*

RONNIE. So it's settled then?

MAC. I can't be sure, Ronnie.

RONNIE. There's very little any of us can be sure of in this life, we know, but, Mac, we met six times last week. Management say they're not yet closing down the garage. Your men are safe, for the moment.

MAC. Ah, but are they? And has management said they're *not* closing down the garage? They've changed the *date* for closure, but *we* asked them to withdraw it.

RONNIE. And haven't they agreed on that?

MAC. The position's very ambiguous.

RONNIE. Industrial disputes usually are, old son.

MAC. Don't be frivolous, brother, the strike threat's not passed yet.

EDITOR'S OFFICE

Editorial continuing.

HARVEY. Right, now, science and politics, how's that coming along?

ANTHONY. Morty's getting a good picture of investments in technology. Should have it by the end of the month.

CHRIS. Norman's pursuing the backbone: 'Has technology rearranged the genes of political issues?' or some such thing to do with futurology.

GORDON. That'll bring them in.

HARVEY. You remain sceptical?

GORDON. I remain sceptical.

MARY. We doing something more about this new book on race by the way?

CHRIS. What do you suggest? Arts reviewed it last week.

MARY. Well, have you read it? I mean just look at this paragraph. It's just such unscientific thinking that makes me so suspicious of the man.

HARVEY. Send someone to interview him, I'd say.

MARY. Ask him if he's erring according to Hudson's law of selective attention to data?

PAUL. That might be a boomerang question, since the journalist's profession is entirely given to just that: the selective attention to data.

BUSINESS NEWS

DOMINIC. They want to take over the shipyards? Workers' control? Right, here's what I'll want to discover:

One: Can it work inherently? i.e. can they produce workers who can manage and administer, men who can overcome demarcation issues and work in a way to double production.

Two: If they can, will it be allowed to work?

Three: If it's not allowed to work will this produce a chain reaction of protest from workers in other industries?

Four: If it *is* allowed to work will it set up a precedent and example to be followed in other industries?

Five: Most important — *how* will it work? That is to say:
         will it work in such a way that it would simply
         produce another hierarchy producing its own set of
         disenchantments.

As a good barrister by training, my questions are already
succinctly formulated.

MORTY. And as a good reporter, the answers already written, I
   trust.

EDITOR'S OFFICE

Editorial continuing.

ANTHONY. And how's Mary's profiles? Coming along, are they?

MARY. Four down, three to go.

ANTHONY. Committing themselves on science versus politics?

MARY. Here and there. George Carron will, of course.

PAUL. I should hope so, being the Minister for Science and
   Technology.

GORDON. Do they actually let you come into their houses,
   fondle their dogs, tickle their grandchildren, pour wine for
   you and all that?

MARY. All that and more.

ANTHONY. More. Ah ha!

MARY. You're a dirty old man, Anthony.

ANTHONY. It's hardly an issue how dirty this old man is.
   Question is, how dirty are they?

MARY. Harvey, I'd like, while we're talking about profiles, to
   pursue someone else I think we should all be keeping an eye on.

PAUL. Morgan King, M.P., no doubt.

HARVEY. Oh, the superstar. I'm lunching with him today.

GORDON. You planning to rubbish him? Poor man. He's only just started his political career. I'd've thought small fry for you, Mary.

PAUL. She's actually been having a go at him for some time.

ANTHONY. Under cover of that 'witty, cool and deathly column' of hers.

HARVEY. They're heathens, Mary, ignore them. Tell us.

MARY. I don't know. He smells phoney.

HARVEY. I'll let you know.

GORDON. Don't his crude honesties appeal to you? You're always complaining about political smoothies.

MARY. I'm just saying he needs to be kept an eye on and I'd like to know you'd be interested if I came up with anything.

HARVEY. Providing we don't get snarled up in any more litigations. Our libel insurance is running low.

GORDON. I actually get prickles on my skin every time I see Mary prepare to lunge for a kill. Thrilling. That's my word for it – thrilling.

MARY. Harvey, would you excuse me? I don't think you need me. *(She leaves.)*

HARVEY. You must stop getting at her or I'll begin to think it's professional jealousy, and you wouldn't want me to think that.

PAUL. I think she's lethal.

CHRIS. But a brilliant journalist.

PAUL. *You* all think so, I know.

POLITICAL AND FEATURES

CYNTHIA. Don't you ever feel uneasy, sometimes, as a journalist? We inundate people with depressing information and they become concerned. Then we offer more information and they become confused. And then we pile on more and more until they feel impotent but we offer them no help. No way out of their feelings of impotence. Don't you ever feel guilty?

NORMAN. Constantly.

PART TWO

THE CENTRE SPACE

Part of the lounge in the home of the Rt Hon. GEORGE CARRON, *Minister for Science and Technology.*
He's playing chess with MARY.

CARRON. I'm a bachelor, Miss Mortimer. If I'd been married — nice cultured woman and all that — I might be more interested in literature, films, plays, all that. But I'm not.

MARY. You don't mind me asking, Mr Carron?

CARRON. After three gruelling sessions with the old man? Ask away. I'll tell you what I mind and don't mind. But art? Can't help you there. You'll have to put me down as illiterate. Science and politics, those are my passions.

MARY. And chess.

CARRON. Ah, chess. My only addiction.

MARY. So, it doesn't worry you that all those upstart writers are required reading in the schools?

CARRON. Worry me?

MARY. After all, *their* values point to one kind of society while you're legislating to shape another kind of society.

CARRON. Worry me? Strange question. Check. Look, I'm an old man and, I'll confess, not a very happy one. I began my career as a Labour politician from a farm labourer's background and half-way changed my politics to Tory — a man's driven by the profit motive, plain and simple, I soon found that out. But, it makes for a lonely life. To be despised. Not nice. You live with it but you never get used to it. Still, that's not the point. What I'm saying is that experience shaped me, not art. I didn't change roads because of what I read in books but because of what I read in man. I don't think I'm a philistine — you mustn't think anything simple like that — but it's — my experience. I'm tone deaf, colour blind and get very impatient with the convenient concoctions literary men make into novels. I saw a play once and I thought to myself, yes, well, them people can behave like that 'cos they got good scripts written for them. I prefer men who write their own scripts. They do it in the House and they do it in the cabinet and they do it at international conferences and that's real. Art shaping society? I doubt it. Science, yes, not books. Still, I've got to believe that, haven't I? Minister for Science and Technology and all that.

MARY. Can we talk about science then?

CARRON. You haven't moved out of check yet.

MARY. Sorry. *(She moves.)*

CARRON. Ah! You know what you're about, don't you?

MARY. I've got three children who kept calling me bourgeois for playing bridge so I pacified them by learning chess.

CARRON. My one great regret — no children. Watch out for your queen.

MARY. The editor wants to focus on the science-versus-politics debate.

CARRON. Facile divisions. Journalese. Look, the argument goes like this, I know it: there develops, it is said, unnoticed by most of us, a whole range of scientific and technological discovery and invention which creeps up behind societies and suddenly—is there! And each time it happens, the argument goes, then all the moral, religious and political deliberations of decades are rendered useless and we have to begin to formulate our opinions all over again. Right? That's the thesis. And it's one that presents this image of a silent, modest, effective activity—science—alongside a vociferous, self-important and ineffectual babelising—politics! It's an attractive picture. I can see why people fall for it and I can see why newspapers choose it as a popular controversy ripe for over-simplification. But how accurate is it? How helpful is it? Look at the period between 1900 and 1913, 'La Belle Époque' we call it. World-wide economic growth, prosperity, scientific and technological advances. The lot!

MARY. And all based on the political and philosophical assumptions of the enlightenment.

CARRON. Right! You've got it!

MARY. Science made possible by politics, not in conflict with it.

CARRON. Exactly! But look what happened after 1913 — something no scientific progress nor philosophical enlightenment can account for nor, I may add, need account for—an idiotic, soul-destroying world war!

MARY. Then who should account for it?

CARRON. Ah! Now you're asking a question which needs the kind of complex answers newspapers can't give and presumably didn't give in those early 1900s. Instead they over-simplified, as you're trying to do. And *they* led to World War One and you and your editor—well, I won't be so presumptuous. Books! History! The interaction of ideas — that's where you'll find your answers and where I think you ought to guide your readers for their answers.

MARY. But, Minister, that's a contradiction. You said *experience* changed men, not ideas from books. Now you're saying certain *ideas* formed the basis for 'La Belle Époque'.

CARRON. Contradictions? Well, you've got to live with them also. A Jewish M.P. once told me a story about an old rabbi who was asked to settle a dispute between two men. The first man tells his version and the rabbi listens, thinks, and says: 'You know, you're right.' Then the second man presents his side of the argument and the rabbi listens, thinks and says: 'You know, you're right.' At which the rabbi's pupil who was standing by waiting for wisdom says: 'But, Rabbi, first you said this man was right, then you said that man was right. How can that be?' And the rabbi listened and thought and said: 'You know what? You're also right.'

ARTS PAGES

SEBASTIAN. Just listen to this, gentlemen. A letter infinitely superior to most. 'Whatever your decision it's bound to prove expensive. If you reject my offering, you will discover very soon, as I have already warned you, that you have missed "the scoop of the century". If you accept it and publish the articles I shall expect payment at a rate that will enable me to complete my life's work during the next two or three years.'

JOHN. Obviously we should buy them. I find it a very touching letter.

SEBASTIAN. I find it intimidating.

ERNST. I find it embarrassing. Reminds me of all those letters I used to write to editors of literary magazines offering, with great benevolence, my very bad poetry.

IN DEPTH

JULIAN. We were at this party and this Tory bag came up to me and she asked me what I did, so I said, despite my extremely youthful looks, I said: 'I edit the *Sunday Paper*, ma'am.' And she, ignoring my youthful looks, believed me and whispered: 'Ah ha! Wanted to meet you. *I* think you've got three fully paid-up members of the Communist Party on your In Depth team.' And quick as a flash I said: 'Oh no, ma'am, they're not as right-wing as all that!'

BUSINESS NEWS

MORTY. But much more important than your controlling shareholder, your *rentier*, was your poor little swindled punter. The big boys *deserve* all they get — trying to make money work for them instead of working for themselves.

EDITOR'S OFFICE

PAUL *visiting*.

PAUL. I'm not happy about our attitude to the government, Harvey. I know you feel we should be more vigorous in our comments but we do stand for something, you know.

HARVEY. Not uncritically, Paul. You can't say we're irresponsible in our condemnations of government policy. It's not the old days. We've got a first-class team. Oxbridge firsts, good, hard analytical brains who understand the problems and—

PAUL.—and nothing, Harvey. They understand nothing. *We* stopped believing in the sanctity of print long ago, but not them. You know and I know and anyone who's an old hand knows that newspapers can't deal in truths but only in facts. Not this lot though. They actually imagine they're trafficking in truth. No humility. But we *can* deal in attitudes and principles and judgments and I think we're betraying this paper's image.

HARVEY. I don't think that's fair, Paul. They're aware of limitations and are very properly careful in their judgments. We'd do the same if the left were in power.

PAUL. I know that, Harvey. But not everyone else on the staff knows it. They're a bit cynical these youngsters you've gathered round you. They see the *Sunday Paper* being an old conservative family newspaper and therefore commanding more credibility, as being the best journal through which to infiltrate radical views. True! The very words they use. 'Infiltrate radical views'.

HARVEY. Come now, Paul, don't let's get too portentous. It'll take more than a few brilliant left-wing journalists to crack the ramifications of this country's deeply entrenched and very, very competitive spirit.

BUSINESS NEWS

ANTHONY (*reading and laughing at a newspaper report*). We're being told here by the illustrious *Telegraph* that—and I quote: 'The Business News section of the *Sunday Paper* is like the TV power game programmes, tending to see all business as a jungle and all business men as nasty, wrangling, grinning, smooth hand-shaking, back-stabbing villains … '

DOMINIC. Except Arnold Weinstock, of course.

NEWS ROOM

HARRY *(on the phone, but first to* MARTIN*)*. The Angry Brigade have struck again, a boutique. *(Into phone)* Let's get this straight. They put a bomb in the boutique, gave them ten minutes to clear out and sent this note to *The Times*? O.K. let's have it. *(Writing down.)* 'If you are not busy being born you are busy buying.' Yes. 'In fashion as in everything else capitalists can only look backwards … ' Jesus! This is school kid's stuff. O.K., go on. 'The future is ours.' Yes. 'Life is so boring there is nothing to do except … ' Except *what*? Spend our wages on *what*? 'Nothing to do except spend our wages on the latest skirt or shirt.' They call this political analysis? It's self-pity. Yes, alright, go on. 'Brothers, sisters, what are your real desires?' Yes. 'Sit in the drug store, look distant, empty, bored … ' Yes, I've got it. Or *what*? 'Or blow it up or burn it down.' Yes. 'You cannot reform profit, capitalism and inhumanity, just kick it till it breaks.' *What*? Revolution? It just ends like that? Revolution? 'Re-vol-u-tion.' Got it. No, I don't write shorthand. I find most people so boring in what they say that my slow longhand is fast enough to catch what's worthwhile. Thanks. *(Replaces receiver.)*

MARTIN. A bomb in a boutique? Jesus! I wish I could distinguish between their outrage and their envy.

FOREIGN DEPT.

Urgent sound of 'tick-tack'.
MARY *and* TAMARA *are reading what is coming through the telex machine.*

MARY. Where the hell is our fiery socialist speaking from now.

TAMARA. Hamburg.

MARY. And what's our superstar doing there?

TAMARA. Some exchange they have with New Lannark.

MARY. He's every bloody where. Read it out, there's a dear.
    (*Phone rings. It's* HARVEY.)

HARVEY. Mary? I want you to look after Peter's affairs for the month he's away.

MARY. And who'll look after mine?

HARVEY. Come on, love, you know you've always wanted to be Special Features editor and you've got the biggest shoulders of any of us.

MARY. Very flattering.

HARVEY. And the sharpest intellect. There! That better?

MARY. By the way, Harvey, isn't it about time Paul was pensioned off?

HARVEY. That question discredits you. I'll forget you asked it.

MARY. He's tired, sentimental and a third-rate mind.

HARVEY. He's efficient, dependable and knows the job from top to bottom. I don't like sacking old men.

MARY. If I'm to cover up for Pete he'll get in my way.

HARVEY. You're relentless, Mary.

MARY. A quality you not infrequently rely upon. Are you free?

HARVEY. No.

MARY. I want to hear your impressions of Morgan King.

HARVEY. Ten minutes. *(Phones down)*

TAMARA. There's something unhealthy about your dislike of Morgan King.

MARY. I can't stand do-gooders. They talk with such pity.

TAMARA. Oh, come now. Every politician is a do-gooder.

MARY. I can't bear to be so sorried for. Please, read it, Tamara.

TAMARA. It's difficult to see where it begins. *(Reading from long, white telex sheet.)* 'I tell you of these incidents in my private life because, if we're talking about the need for society to produce the whole man then let *us* be seen as whole men, imperfections and all, since it is an imperfect man for whom we must build a compassionate society.'

MARY. Really! Who does he think he is? Protesting his imperfections as though we wouldn't believe he had any in the first place. Don't you find something irritating about a good person?

TAMARA. Not just 'something'. It's perfectly easy to identify: their goodness, by comparison, reveals our shabbiness. Simple!

(MARY, exasperated, leaves.)

SPORTS PAGES

MARVIN. I've got eight brothers and they've all, all of them got funny names. Like Jack the Corporation, James the Jumper, Willie the Woodman. And why? Because my parents were publicans and each of us was born in a different pub. Solly the Dun Cow, Chris the Mortar and Pestle, Horace the Mulberry Bush. It was Jonah the Pig and Whistle who used to object most.

RONNIE. And you, Marvin. What were you called?

MARVIN. Don't laugh. Marvin the Mermaid.

NEWS ROOM

MARTIN. And yet, you know, I've a sneaking sympathy for the Angry Brigade. There's something about ostentation makes you want to blow it up.

HARRY. It's their warm and cosy world of small sabotage that irritates me.

MARTIN. Do you know I saw a Rolls-Royce with a TV aerial on it today?

HARRY. And their weakness for simplified political platitudes.

MARTIN. Why should anyone want to watch TV while being driven through interesting streets or countryside.

HARRY. I mean they're just spit-and-run boys, aren't they?

MARTIN. Pale blue it was. And I was confused between admiration for its mechanics and disgust for its opulence. And as I was driving I got this great urge to crash into it. Irrational really. Not an urge I was proud of. Bit mean. Unworthy.

HARRY. Anyway, I think their passion for destruction is inherited from the very enemy they think they loathe. Relieves them of tiny angers.

MARTIN. Still, I did *so* want to knock it down.

HARRY. And they're no more a match for the lovely, seductive philosophical defences of capitalism than their do-it-yourself bombs are a match for tanks and nuclear toys.

MARTIN. Still, they have tried everything else without much effect. Marches, sit-downs, teach-ins, civil disobedience.

SPORTS PAGES

RONNIE. We used to have a woman on the travel page who regularly, for two years, used to hand in stuff saying such and such a place was a lovely sunny beach until the Jews got there! Didn't care that it was never printed, she never seemed to get the message. And it took two years before management could bring themselves to sack her. She was a widow, you see. Lived alone. Cruelly abandoned by kith and kin. Acid personality—but a loner. You can't fling people on the dole just 'cos they're anti-semitic, can you?

MARVIN. No sense of revenge, that's what irritates me about you Jews. Understanding of everything and everyone. Not healthy, Ronnie boy. Bite! Gotta bite back.

RONNIE. That's our trouble. We're beginning to.

BUSINESS NEWS

CHRIS *visiting*.

DOMINIC (*to* MORTY). And who's your Arnold Weinstock for this month?

MORTY. Oh, he'll last, my son. Good for a reference every two months or so—at least.

ANTHONY (*to* CHRIS). And what are our In-depth colleagues in-depthing this week?

CHRIS. The crash of boring old bridges, I'm afraid.

ANTHONY. And what help can we offer you on that?

CHRIS. Not crashing bridges, old son, but crashing insurance companies.

C

ANTHONY. Ah! The ill-fated Atlantis company.

CHRIS. I've got a lead from a high-up on the Board of Trade.

DOMINIC *(mocking)*. 'At 08.00 hrs the shrewd and enigmatic Mr Cruikshank —'

MORTY *(taking up the mockery)*. '—a clean-shaven, handsome man, greying attractively at the temples —'

DOMINIC. '—was seen by his cleaner to arrive an hour earlier than usual at the head office of Atlantis Insurance —'

MORTY. '—Meanwhile, back at the Board of Trade, Mr X —'

DOMINIC. '—who shall remain nameless —'

MORTY. '—was heard cracking his hard-boiled, mid-morning egg —'

DOMINIC. '—four minutes, of course —'

MORTY. '—with greater anxiety than usual —'

DOMINIC. '—At that moment, 800 miles away in the Bahamas, the beautiful wife of the Swiss ambassador was sun-bathing with the even more beautiful wife of the junior partner of Atlantis Insurance and discussing the latest wines of the little-known but highly sought after Château de Montaigne —'

MORTY. '—At first sight all these far-flung incidents have no connection —'

CHRIS. Care to take over our column, boys?

ANTHONY. Oh, we're much too flippant for your serious investigations, Chris. Now —

CHRIS. Now. What's the percentage an insurance company must set aside to cover claims?

ANTHONY. Well, let's see. The big boys arrange that sort of thing amongst themselves, you know.

CHRIS. Good God!

ANTHONY. Yes, God is good. But, it would appear, only to them what already have! Now, at one time it was 9% and then ...

FOREIGN DEPT.

GORDON. Of course you're growing old. We're all growing old. Especially in this profession. At 32 we're old already.

TAMARA. Gordon, can you lend me a couple of pounds, please?

GORDON *(while dipping into his pocket)*. I remember when Kruschev died, there was this reporter, one of our top men, tried to phone through to the Kremlin. Didn't stop to think that neither of them would be able to speak the other's language, just automatically reached for the phone. The spark goes. Last night on TV I was watching the awful tragedy of the three Russian astronauts dying in space and I was thinking — yes, now how can we handle that? This way? Yes, maybe. That way? Yes, well — I'll sleep on it. Years ago I'd have immediately rung up people and started generating ideas.

TAMARA *(referring to newspaper)*. And the slaughter goes on. 'West Pakistan tanks fire on university students asleep in their dormitories.' We're not reporting foreign news, we're reporting madness.

POLITICAL AND FEATURES

NORMAN *exercising with chest expanders.*

CYNTHIA. I find your piece on futurology spine-chilling.

NORMAN. Brilliantly written though.

CYNTHIA. What's so depressing about the futurologists is their way of wrapping up the future. They define it so precisely that they obliterate it. There *is* no future. They've brought it up to the present. Nothing to look forward to or be spontaneous about.

NORMAN *(puffing)*. You miss the point. They don't define what *will* happen — only what *could* happen. Know the dangers — prevent them.

CYNTHIA. But they don't make judgments about their predictions.

NORMAN. Not their job.

CYNTHIA. Why not add a para and say that?

NORMAN *(pause in exercising)*. Because I've got a para which, if you read carefully, points out that they'd developed a unique method of formulating a question which combines science with its moral implications.

CYNTHIA. Example?

NORMAN. Example: Politicians know the potential of scientific and medical research in the field of mind control. Question: should legislation be passed to control the mind controllers before perfection of technique makes its misuse too tempting to resist? *(Continues exercise.)*

*(*RONNIE *enters.)*

RONNIE. What the hell good do you think you're doing?

NORMAN. Healthy body, healthy mind.

RONNIE. What great writer do *you* know who ran a couple of miles before picking up a pen?

NORMAN *(puffing)*. Walk, swim, feel fresher, prepared for anything.

RONNIE. If you're an idiot, mate, not even an Olympic medal can change that. A lovely bit of private distress, that'll sharpen your wits, not a handful of jerks.

NORMAN *(stopping)*. I'm not suggesting a healthy body *makes* a healthy mind, but given a lively mind to begin with —

CYNTHIA. — such as you've got —

NORMAN. — such as I've got, then it's enhanced by a fit body. Oh my God! I've strained a shoulder muscle.

IN DEPTH

JULIAN. What are the layabouts in our Business section up to?
CHRIS. Oh, trying to find a new Arnold Weinstock to write up.
JULIAN. In order to knock down —
CHRIS. — to make room for another Arnold Weinstock to build up —
JULIAN. — in order to knock down —
CHRIS. — to make room for another —

BUSINESS NEWS

MORTY. Have you seen the new poster of Chairman Mao hanging up in the In Depth offices?
ANTHONY. It's rather like the photographs of nudes which boys hang in their rooms at public school to assert their independence while temporarily trapped by the enemy.

IN DEPTH

CHRIS. I *do* want a cigarette. I *don't* want a cigarette. (*Reaching for phone and cigarettes.*) I *do* want a cigarette. (*Reaching for a bottle of beer.*) And a drink. Bloody bridges!

ARTS PAGES

SEBASTIAN. You actually think Hughie Green is a genius?

JOHN. Yes, I do — and I chose the word carefully.

SEBASTIAN. And how would your article on him set about proving that extraordinary misuse of the epithet?

JOHN. Figures. His television parlour games have the highest ratings.

SEBASTIAN. Oh, I see. Impressed by numbers, are you?

JOHN. *And* he's a man of the people.

SEBASTIAN. Is that his claim or your conclusion?

ERNST. But his gags are terrible.

JOHN. Which is precisely what puts him on a level with 25 million viewers who are desperately relieved to hear a famous man only able to make jokes as awful as they would themselves.

ERNST. And *that's* genius?

JOHN. There's more. He's interested in the trivia of living without attempting to counsel or instruct. He amplifies the ordinary and gives it status.

SEBASTIAN. Most interesting. You mean he's like politicians who, to curry favour and gain power, stultify the development of mind and personality by applauding the lowest instincts.

JOHN. Depends how you put it. He puts it another way. 'The people count,' he says.

SEBASTIAN. Oh, they all say that, dear fellow.

JOHN. 'The people are the only patrons,' he says. 'I am the public's servant and I am there to do more or less what they want. Why defy those people who are your friends?' However, he makes a brilliant volte face when he defends the establishment. 'I sincerely believe,' he says, 'that there are certain of us who are better equipped to know what is good for us than others.' And double-thinking like that is real genius.

SEBASTIAN. Not in my dictionary it isn't.

IN DEPTH

CHRIS (*on phone*). Professor Cobblestone? Good morning. Chris Mackintosh of the *Sunday Paper* here — yes, you've guessed it, those fallen bridges. No — alright, not now. But in fact I didn't want to go into it *now*, only check you're the right man. You are? Splendid. To be frank, I don't know how to start thinking on this subject at all and — good! I'll ring you again when I've read through all this material and got a basic shape to the piece and ask you if it makes engineering sense. O.K.? Thanks. Bye. (*Replaces receiver. Closes his eyes.*) Do I want a cigarette? No! I don't want a cigarette. (*Picks up phone to dial again.*)

SPORTS PAGES

Phone ringing.

RONNIE. Ron Shapiro here.

(*It's from the editor's office.* HARVEY *has with him* MAC SMITH, *a trade union official.*)

HARVEY. Ron? Look, I've got Mac with me. They're querying the agreement we all thought we came to last week and if it's

not ironed out now we'll all be in the shit again. Can you
come down?

RONNIE. Coming. *(Replaces receiver.)* Who'd be bloody father
of a newspaper chapel!

MARVIN. That stoppage again?

RONNIE. They may freeze the messengers. Ring round, get copy
telephoned straight through to here and bypass copy takers. I
shouldn't as a union official, but fuck it! I want the paper to
come out and I don't care. You agree?

MARVIN. Agreed.

　　　*(*RONNIE *makes his way to editor's office.)*

IN DEPTH

JULIAN *(on phone)*. Look, I'm a layman and so if I could explain
in layman's language why those bridges fell, rather than in
your expertise — yes? Good. As I understand it it goes something like this: I build shelves for 15lb jam jars, test the shelves
by putting 20lb jam jars on, use 15lb jam jars for 20 years and
then return to 20lb jam jars ... what? Oh, I see. Jam jars are
hardly applicable. Of course. Well, let's start again ...

POLITICAL AND FEATURES

CYNTHIA *(on phone)*. Yes, well, I think it's a very interesting
story, workers *should* get a day off on their birthday, but it's
hardly for us. Try the News Room.

IN DEPTH

CHRIS. As far as I can make out it's a perfectly decent feat of engineering but no one seems to have taken account of the fact that the things are built by incompetent, lumpen Irish labourers who don't care a damn ...

EDITOR'S OFFICE

MAC. You see, Harvey, it says there that we've asked for withdrawal of the decision to close down the garage. Now you know that's not true. *We've* never ever said that. Management shouldn't go around sending notes like this to the staff misrepresenting our case. We've only asked that the *date* of closure be withdrawn to give us a chance to negotiate the men's future. That's not unreasonable, is it?

RONNIE. Hasn't that happened already, Mac?

MAC. Now Ronnie, you *know* it hasn't. They've *changed* the date. Postponed it as it were. But not actually withdrawn it.

HARVEY. Why do you want it withdrawn?

MAC. Now, Harvey, *you* shouldn't be asking questions like that. Supposing we agree to a date for closing down the garages and when that date comes we're not in agreement on redundancy compensation, eh? Come now, Harvey. *You're* an old enough hand.

HARVEY. But for Christ's sake, Mac —

MAC. Now then, Harvey, Harvey. Let's not raise our voices.

HARVEY (*softer*). For Christ's sake, Mac, we're grown up, intelligent human beings. We've had problems like this before. Why *shouldn't* we come to an agreement on redundancy claims in good time?

MAC. Grown up, intelligent human beings — true. But 'the best laid schemes of mice and men' — you know what I mean? Besides, Ronnie, I'll tell *you* the truth. Because this document has falsified our position it's become a matter of principle for us. And for them? For management? Well, they've decided on a date and they've made it a matter of pride not to shift from it. So there's your problem. Principle versus pride. I'm taking it to my head office now and if nothing happens by the end of the week I'm asking them to make the stoppage official and I hope your men'll give us your support. Good day, lads. *(Leaves.)*

RONNIE. Doesn't look like we're going to have a paper this weekend.

HARVEY. I'll bring the fucking thing out, even if it means working the machines on my own and delivering the sheets myself. But I may need a little help from you, Ronnie.

RONNIE. When not?

IN DEPTH

CHRIS. What I can't understand is how they *test* bridges.

JULIAN. They used to get battalions of guards to walk over them, then if the foundations trembled —

CHRIS. Our army isn't big enough, is it?

EDITOR'S OFFICE

MARY *visiting*.

MARY. And what was your lunch like with comrade King?

HARVEY. I can see why you're interested in him. He's a bit too good to be true, isn't he?

MARY. So you agree with me? He should be watched?

HARVEY. Oh come on, Mary. He's not a spy, for God's sake.

MARY. But he's sinister.

HARVEY. He's complex.

MARY. And sinister.

HARVEY. No, guarded.

MARY. Guarded? The opposite! He's *giving*. All the time. Can't stop talking and offering his half-baked opinions on everything.

HARVEY. You underestimate him. He's got a good mind and a generous one. Perceptive too. He sees the scale of problems and, what's more attractive, he sees them in the perspective of history—which always impresses me. No, there's something, something else. Something about the way he talks, as though he only wants to answer the questions *he* asks; as though—I don't know, as though if he stops talking he'll give someone the opportunity to ask the one question he doesn't want to answer.

MARY. As I say, sinister.

HARVEY. No secretive. One very odd thing he said—not odd in its meaning but the words he used. He said: 'One thing I disagree with emphatically is the left's concept of the new man. Dangerous,' he said, 'misleading. It sets stout hearts on to the wrong line of action. It's not the "new man" we must *create*,' he said, 'but the original man we must *reveal*.'

MARY. Sophistry.

HARVEY. 'Clear away the undergrowth of ignorance and the rubble of fear that's gathered around him over the centuries,' he said, 'and when the dust from that job settles, then,' and these are his odd words, 'when the dust from that job settles, then you'll see all the patterns men can make for the pleasure of their living.'

MARY. 'The patterns men can make for the pleasure of their living'. Jesus! Harvey! Come on! They say that certain poets are bullied by a bad conscience — well, this is a conscience bullied by bad poetry.

FOREIGN DEPT.

GORDON. Why don't you take a year off? Write a book? Everyone's doing it.

TAMARA. Write a book? Ha! That's very funny. I can hardly assemble words for the little bits and pieces of so-called foreign commentary they pay me to do here. A book! I'd like to resign.

GORDON. Why don't you?

TAMARA. I write letters of resignation every year. Conveyor-belt work, harsh, destructive, written in a hurry. I'm sick of first-class travel and first-class hotels and the quick friendships with people about whom one has finally to write something unsympathetic. And then when there's a drive to cut expenses in all departments everyone makes a moral pitch to defend their fraudulent demands. Uch! Ugly! Sometimes I think I'm in journalism because I'm unfit for anything else.

NEWS ROOM

SECRETARY *(on the phone)*. A union official who's *what*? Got a clause in about birthdays? No, it's hardly for the News Room. Try our industrial correspondent. You'll find him in Business News.

(HARRY rushes in.)

HARRY. Paul? That hold-up of the supermarket in Bolton?

PAUL. Yes?

HARRY. There's been a new development.

PAUL. What are you doing with a crime story?

HARRY. It may not be a crime story.

PAUL. Not?

HARRY. Not! Three days later 97 old people living in a new development for old-age pensioners woke up and found boxes of groceries on their front-door step.

PAUL. And there's a connection?

HARRY. The police aren't certain. But I've got another hunch I want to follow. Remember that factory manager kidnapped two months ago, the one that had a strike on his hands for being a bully?

PAUL. So?

HARRY. When he was released the strike was over and the men reinstated but none of us, no paper, was able to get a statement from him.

PAUL. Go on.

HARRY. Well, there's another strike in South Wales, place called Llantrisant, and this time it's unofficial and not the manager but the boss himself has been kidnapped.

PAUL. Are you suggesting the unions have become militant urban guerrillas?

HARRY. Not the unions, but someone! Now, there's something else—and here's the real break. Since the kidnapping there's been a large bank robbery and though there's no strike pay the men have been given money.

PAUL. A local strike fund.

HARRY. No! Their *full* wages.

PAUL. How?

HARRY. Cash, in the post.

PAUL. Well, that's the Angry Brigade.

HARRY. No again! The Angry Brigade are bomb throwers not soup kitchens. Besides, they'd announce themselves.

PAUL. Sounds to me as though you'd better consult the brilliant Miss Mortimer. She's got Peter's job for the month.

ARTS PAGES

ERNST. Why do you think the devasting Mary Mortimer has it in for the King of New Lannark?

JOHN. Because she can't bear idealism anywhere but in her own column, where she calls it 'responsibility', while in anyone else it's called 'charlatanism'.

SEBASTIAN. No, no, no! You mustn't talk to him so glibly or he'll put us into one of his novels. We—and she—are much more complex than that. She suffers from the schizophrenia we all suffer from. She can't bear people who make judgments and since, in attacking them, *she* has to judge, therefore she's torn all ends up.

ERNST. But we all make judgments, surely.

JOHN. Only we fear to be seen doing so.

SEBASTIAN. Precisely! It's like a dirty act, to be done in secrecy. If you make a judgment you seem, by your choice, to be indicting those who've not chosen as you've done. *We* know about it because we work in a department where the greatest intimidations of all operate. Whether they like it or not most men regard the artist in fear, as a kind of magic man who can see the truth behind the façade, the devil in the making. And Mr Morgan King is a working-class politician who — to his credit, I may add — has innocently stumbled upon the truth of art. Terrible presumption! Frightfully difficult to tolerate. Of course, to be the artist himself is the greatest presumption of all, but sometimes they let *him* get away with it. What they can't bear are lay enthusiasts like Morgan King trying to encourage *others* to pursue the bad habits of art. That's his great sin. 'Go to your artists,' he cries, 'don't listen to us, we're too jaundiced!' 'You're imposing your tastes on us,' they scream back at him from the barricades of democracy, as though social relations didn't involve impositions of some kind or another. Or their favourite paroxysm of rage: 'You're taking culture to the masses!' as though to *take* anything to people were somehow more sinister than to *sell* it to them. Capital fellow! Doomed, of course. And then he confuses his enemies — and this is why Mary Mortimer can't forgive him because she'd like to have said it herself — he confuses them by making outrageous demands such as that old age pensioners should get what the national minimum wage is, and that all laws should be whittled down to the absolute essentials. Fools! I don't personally have much sympathy for the giant-killing Miss Mortimers of this world nor that 'witty, cool and deathly column' of hers.

POLITICAL AND FEATURES

HARRY *visiting*.

MARY. You've done no investigating yourself?

HARRY. No, just assembled cuttings and kept an eye on it.

MARY. And the sequence is: a supermarket hold-up, distribution of food to old age pensioners, strike in Wales and a bank robbery?

HARRY. And then *full* strike pay.

MARY. And *then* full strike pay. Um. And we know it's not the Angry Brigade?

HARRY. Certain.

MARY. What's your hunch?

HARRY. It's only a hunch.

MARY. Let's hear it.

HARRY. And it's way out.

MARY. Stop covering your retreats, out with it.

HARRY. An opposition secret society.

MARY. That's not way out. There must be people in this green and pleasant land simply livid that they're not Uruguayan Tupamaros.

HARRY. Exactly! They must be intellectuals.

NORMAN. Easy! Some of my best friends are intellectuals.

HARRY. They're highly organised, sophisticated, a sense of humour and, probably, opposed to violence.

MARY. And what do you propose?

HARRY. This: I've made contact with the Angry Brigade. They're amateurs, clumsy and highly emotional. Now, if such a secret society does exist they're bound, sooner or later, to want to make contact with the Angries to tell them to lay off the bombings.

MARY. Not sure I accept the logic of that. Still—
HARRY. I just want one week free from other assignments.
MARY. I think we can spare him.
    (HARRY leaves.)

WOMEN'S PAGES

JANE. How about a series on people's obsessions?
ANGELA. Do *you* have obsessions?
JANE. Me? I don't know.
ANGELA. And would you confess them?
JANE. Depends what I discovered I was obsessed with.
ANGELA. No, I prefer the idea of a series on 'my best friend'.
    Find out what human qualities the famed and renowned look
    for in their closest.
    (Pause.)
JANE. People sitting around in offices, lost, that's all a newspaper
    is, sitting around waiting for ideas to come, wondering what
    the hell to do next.

THE CENTRE SPACE

MARY MORTIMER's *lounge.*
*Her three children—*AGNES, JONATHAN *and* DESMOND—*have
come for a monthly 'family dinner'.*
MARY *is in the kitchen preparing the meal.* JONATHAN *is reading
from a sheet of copy. It's a proof of* MARY's *current column.*

JONATHAN. She's attacking him again.

DESMOND. Read it.

AGNES. But please, let's not quarrel this time?

JONATHAN (reading). 'Mr Morgan-fiery-socialist-M.P.-King is with us once more. Oh, what a dear, human, compassionate philosopher we have in our midst. And how thankful we must be, as he constantly reminds us, to have such a learned member of parliament guiding us through the confusions of such awful times.'

DESMOND. *Does* he 'constantly remind us?'

AGNES. It's mother's poetic licence to lie.

JONATHAN. 'We quote: "I believe," says the self-styled sage, "that the first great myth of all time was the story of the creation of order out of chaos, and all men's greatest endeavours since then have been the re-enactment of that one first myth. The universe is self-perpetuating and that means chaos. And, in it all, man has but one task: to create order and understanding if and wherever he can. And because the chaos is endless so man's task will be endless. And if there is a purpose in life *that* is it, and that is all it is." Unquote.'

AGNES. I can remember when he first said that.

JONATHAN. 'We may not know what he means,' says our oh so witty mother, 'but it's certainly reassuring to have such serious sounding pontifications as this to pin by our bedside and read each night before pulling sleep over our troubled eyes in this troubled world.'

(JONATHAN *has beside him a portable tape-recorder the button of which he now presses to produce the sound of an audience whistling and applauding loudly. He throws his arms open as though presenting this extract to 'an audience' for their acclaim. The recorder is his latest 'toy' and he'll do this every so often throughout the scene.*)

DESMOND. They all write so badly, that's what's so depressing.

JONATHAN. Their biggest mistake is to quote the people they

want to demolish. Always boomerangs. Much better than their own little fifth-form farts. How about that? 'You've had the Barretts of Wimpole Street and now we bring to your screens — da-dum — The Little Farts of Fleet Street'. *(Presses tape for 'applause'.)*

AGNES *(unwrapping a package)*. But no quarrels. Jonathan?

JONATHAN. Yes, elder sister.

AGNES. We only have dinner with her once a month so no more dreary taunts about her being bourgeois. Yes?

DESMOND *(deep in newspaper)*. Yes, elder sister.

AGNES. We don't think much of her column but we love her. Understood?

TOGETHER. Yes, elder sister.

AGNES *(revealing a Hogarth print in frame)*. Think she'll like it?

(JONATHAN presses tape to applaud print.)

DESMOND. Is that genuine?

AGNES. Not your first edition, of course. From a late edition, possibly the fourth, 1838, or thereabouts. Bought it from a half-hour conversationalist.

DESMOND. A what?

AGNES. The dealer. Sweet man. But you can't talk to him for very long. He's so used to selling paintings and prints for which it's only necessary to switch on his brilliance and charm for thirty minutes — customers can't stay longer, you see — that it's become a habit with him. Shines for half an hour and then he recedes. Can't help himself. Depresses him no end.

(MARY enters in apron with a tray containing pot of 'stew', plates and cutlery. She plonks it on table, lifts lid triumphantly and waits for response. JONATHAN switches on tape of applause.)

MARY. My God! It's going to be one of those evenings.

(They all begin to help themselves. Then —)

Well, talk to me, my children. I know we always end up

quarrelling over politics but that's no reason to be terrified of telling me your professional gossip. *(All three start at once.)* Whoa! Jonathan, 'the youngest'. You start.

JONATHAN. Directed my first concert.

MARY. Great mistake to televise concerts.

JONATHAN. Agree.

MARY. Good God! We've started with agreements.

JONATHAN. Have you noticed how, at concerts, there are always one or two who leap to applaud almost before the last note has been struck? And you never know whether they do it from enthusiasm or from a wish to get it in that they know the piece so well.

> *(Silence. There seems nothing to add or go on to from there.*
> JONATHAN *presses recorder for his own applause.)*

MARY. We'll try the scientist then.

DESMOND. Three Soviet scientists — G. I. Beridze, G. R. Macharashvili and L. M. Mosulishvili — have discovered gold in wine.

MARY. I beg your pardon?

DESMOND. Flowers and plants, you see, contain in their tissues residues of the metals contained in the soil where they grow. Hence bio-chemistry can trace deposits of nickel, silver, copper, cobalt, uranium, lead and other metals by pursuing, picking and analysing flowers and fruit.

> *(Silence.)*

And so three Soviet scientists called G. I. Beridze, G. R. Macharashvili and L. M. Mosulishvili have discovered gold in wine. *(Pause)* Which comes from grapes. *(Pause)* Which grows in soils.

> *(Silence.)*

Well, don't I get a round of applause for that?

> *(*JONATHAN *belatedly switches on tape.)*

MARY. Do you children rehearse your pieces before coming to dine with me?

AGNES. This is a very fine stew, mother.

MARY. There speaks the diplomat of the family. How's the foreign office?

JONATHAN. Mother, don't be so damned bourgeois. We don't *have* to make conversation.

AGNES *(forestalling friction)*. I might be posted to the embassy in Lagos.

MARY. If he calls me bourgeois again I'll —

AGNES. I'll know in a month's time.

(Silence.)

MARY. Bloody hell! You're not the most comfortable family to sit down to eat a meal with. Why must you always make me feel I've done something to feel guilty for?

JONATHAN. It's a change from you making others feel guilty in your columns.

MARY. That's my job. Investigation! Democratic scrutiny!

(JONATHAN presses tape for applause.)

And turn that bloody machine off! *(Pause)* Oh, go home. I swear, I always swear I'll never make these dinners again and each time I relent, each time I think — no! They won't get at me this time, it'll be a happy family event. And each time it happens again. What do I need it for?

AGNES. We're sorry.

MARY. Don't I have enough bloody headaches in that bloody newspaper office and those stupid, vain, self-opinionated people I have to interview?

JONATHAN. You can't exactly deride those you interview as 'self-opinionated' when those interviews appear in a column called 'Opinions'.

MARY. Oh, can't I just?

DESMOND. Mary, why have you got your teeth into Morgan King?

MARY. Morgan King? What the hell do you care about Morgan King?

AGNES. Desmond, you promised.

MARY. Why Morgan King and none of the others?

DESMOND. It's just that a special kind of savagery comes out with him and it shows.

MARY. I'm a savage columnist, didn't you know?

DESMOND. We're embarrassed, that's all.

MARY. Oh no, you're not. There's a reason. Why Morgan King?

AGNES. He conducted a series of seminars on local authorities at Jonathan's college in Oxford and we all got to know him rather well, that's all.

MARY. Well, why didn't I get to hear about him? I knew all your other friends from university.

DESMOND. Other students, yes; but we kept the tutors and visiting lecturers to ourselves.

MARY. I don't believe you.

AGNES. This is silly. Of course it's not only Morgan King, it's your column in general. We feel it's getting —

DESMOND. — bitchy —

AGNES. — no —

JONATHAN. — strident. That's the word. (*Presses tape for applause.*)

MARY. Please, please, PLEASE don't push that fucking button again.

JONATHAN. Now don't cry, mother. Tough journalists don't cry.

MARY. You're rather cruel children, aren't you?

DESMOND (*shamefaced*). Yes, we are, you're right. I'm sorry.

AGNES. We're all sorry. Look, the stew's getting cold.

MARY. Well, fuck the stew! You don't get off as easily as that.

JONATHAN. Always dangerous to apologise. The bourgeoisie has its sting in the 'tail of its tears'. Mao?

MARY. I AM NOT BOURGEOIS! Bourgeois is a state of mind not of wealth.

JONATHAN. Not in the classic sense it's not.

MARY. To hell with the classic sense. Words acquire new meanings. Think! you have to *think* about them. Your lot are so bloody mindless. *(With forced calm and mounting distress)* I love and care for my children. That's natural, an old, old cycle, tested *long* before men began exploiting men. If I'd forced you into professions you'd've been miserable with, if I'd have given you luxuries to soften the spirit of your spine *that* would have been bourgeois. But what's my crime? To give you a home to dig your personalities in; security! Not to seclude you but to help you face an insecure world. That's not bourgeois — well, is it? I'm not bourgeois if I enjoy the best that men have fought to preserve from the past — only if I allow that past to cripple the future. I'm not bourgeois if I enjoy comfort — only if comfort defuses my anger against injustice. I'm not bourgeois if I acknowledge a debt to dead men and if I'm fearful of the future. That's human. To *enjoy* being helpless about evil, *that's* bourgeois, but to *feel*, to just simply *feel* helpless about evil, that's human. To have loves and hates and failures and regrets and nostalgias, that's human. If I pretend order exists when it doesn't, *that's* bourgeois, but if I try to create order out of the chaos of my miserable life, that's human, bloody human, bloody bloody human.

(AGNES picks up the proof of MARY's column and gently offers it to her.)

AGNES. You see, mother, he also talks about order out of chaos. That's just what we mean. It's as though you're fighting yourself, and it shows. In your column it shows. *(Pause)* Mary, we're our mother's children. *(Small laugh)* No escaping.

(MARY is stung but it only adds to deepen her distress.)

Look. A Hogarth print. We've bought you a present.

ACT II

PART THREE

THE CENTRE SPACE

An arbour in the grounds of the home of the Chancellor of the Exchequer,
SIR REGINALD MACINTYRE.
He is strolling up and down with MARY.

MARY. And the final question, Sir Reginald.

MACINTYRE. You won't be offended if I say, thank God!

MARY. Three days is a long time, I know. You've been very
patient. It's a very personal one. I've asked each minister this
and told them they can answer or tell me to go to hell.

MACINTYRE. I'm not very good at saying such things to ladies
but I hope your question doesn't tempt me too much.

MARY. It's this. How do you reconcile the needs of your own
private standards of living with the needs of those working
people whose standards of living you, as Chancellor, are in
office to regulate. *(Long pause)* Please, if you think it too
impertinent.

MACINTYRE. Impertinent? Yes, I suppose I do find it that.
(Pause) Do you mind if I answer in an oblique way, without,
I trust, being evasive? *(Pause)* It's a terrible problem, democracy. You see, if we could turn round and say all the men
who are dustmen are dustmen because of their inequality of
opportunity then it would be easy. No problem. We would
simply create the right opportunity. But it's not so, is it?
Make *opportunity* equal and the inequality of their qualities
soon becomes apparent. It's a cruel statement to make but
men are dustmen or lavatory attendants or machine minders

or policemen because of intellectual limitations. There! Does
that offend you? It used to offend me. Most unpalatable view
of human beings. But all my encounters with them point to
that fact. Even if we automate all sewage, everything, we're
still confronted with the awful fact that some men *are* born
with intellectual limitations. Now, what do we do? We can't
talk of these things, it's taboo. We can't say in public 'some
men are less intelligent than others' — though it's part of any
discussion on democracy. So what *should* we do? Help them
forget by compensating them for their inadequacies with
large pay packets? But what of the worker whose intellect is
not so limited and who feels he should be paid higher for
those abilities? Shall we tell him such distinctions are invalid?
Shall we say 'a man's a man for all that'? Lovely sentiments.
How I wish I could say them every day to myself, to my
friends, to my constituents. But it's not even true for the
dustman. Because when he strikes for more pay he may not
be asking to be paid for his ability or responsibilities but he *is*
asking to be paid for doing what other men *don't want to do*.
For what I think should be named 'the undesirability factor'.
Isn't *that* a distinction? And a very intimidating distinction, I
may add. In democracies those who do our dirty work have
us these days by, as they say, the short and curlies. Now,
government must, you'll agree, remain in civilised hands. So,
whose 'short and curlies' should civilised man hold on to?

MARY. Perhaps it's the mark of the civilised man that he disdains
from holding on to anyone's 'short and curlies'.

MACINTYRE. No. Only that he *appears* not to be doing so. Does
that also shock you? You probably despise appearances. But
wouldn't you consider me boorish if I spoke to a simple man
in a way that showed him I *thought* he was simple? Wouldn't
you expect of me a politeness, a civility, a humanity to show
him respect by *not* discussing with him what I thought was

beyond his intellect or asking him to perform duties beyond his power? Surely you'd want me to *appear* to be his equal, which I could only do by not frustrating or humiliating him in that way.

MARY. But supposing your judgments are wrong? Supposing the man is capable of more than you give him credit for?

MACINTYRE. Supposing all our judgments are wrong? Yours of me, mine of you—so? Do we cease making them? We are appointed because our judgments are more often right than wrong. That too is one of the risks of democracy, unless you can find me a man who can create a system—or a system which can create a man—whose judgment is right, all the time, about everything. Am I making myself clear?

MARY. Perfectly.

MACINTYRE. Do you find an answer shaping in all that? *(Pause)* You will, of course, let me see the typescript before going into print?

EDITOR'S OFFICE

An editorial conference.

GORDON. Well, do we have a newspaper this week or not?

ANTHONY. The problem, old friend, lies in the difference between the production side and the creative side. We're prepared to work at all hours in order to get a newspaper out and production doesn't care a damn about the kind of journalism we think we produce. And why should they? They don't read it.

GORDON. You think it would make much difference if they did?

HARVEY. Thirty-three garage men now, compensation, facilities for retraining—or 2,500 losing their jobs in a few years' time. Those are the alternatives but they can't see it. That's what gets me.

GORDON. *There's* your technology-versus-politics problem, Harvey. Right in your own back yard.

ANTHONY. And a back yard it *is*—*that's* the problem. We've got Victorian machinery. Thousands to man it. Millions to buy it. Six years to install it. And all you really need is £100,000 for a web-offset machine and a handful of typists to run it instead of expensive, obsolete printing men. Of *course* you'll always have stoppages.

HARVEY. Anyway gentlemen, it's in the hands of their head office and our management boys—let them fight it out and may the best man win. Now. The Indo-Pakistan war. What about *that* bloody mess?

BUSINESS NEWS

DOMINIC. Well, people who fuck up the system appeal to me.
(Phone rings. He picks it up. It's MARTIN *from News Room.)*

MARTIN. Dom? I've just had an earbending fink on the phone who says he's got damaging documents implicating Leonard Crafton.

DOMINIC. Head of Onyx Foods? Oh, a charming man, a con but charming. Everyone wants to rubbish him.

MARTIN. Will you see him?

DOMINIC. If we must.

MARTIN. He sounds interesting if erroneous.

DOMINIC. Interesting if erroneous. I'll remember that.

EDITOR'S OFFICE

Editorial continuing.

HARVEY. And as far as I can see we're going to be the only ones to give the cholera epidemic a big spread. The dailies have hardly touched it. Map with arrows showing its route, three nine-inch columns — front page.

ANTHONY. Don't believe in epidemic scares personally. The agencies always launch them with mortality figures in the hundreds and two days later whittle them down to ten. But if *you* think it's a real danger —

GORDON. *You* don't believe in the pollution scare either, so you're no judge.

ANTHONY. Pollution's different.

HARVEY. Which nicely brings me to my next point. I want to cover the Mersey, long diagram, showing who's pouring what into its waters and from where. Every firm named, questioned, challenged.

WOMEN'S PAGES

ANGELA *(reading a women's magazine)*. Ooooh! Look! Moira Hartnel's entered the battle for women's liberation.

JANE. A top model gone politicking?

ANGELA. Think she's worth pursuing?

JANE. Any staying power?

ANGELA. We only have to do her once. She's not *star* quality.

JANE. Thank God for the woman's magazine. Can always rely on them to fill a hole in the column.

ANGELA. How about 'From women's waists to wasted women'?

JANE. Or 'Model mauls men'?

ANGELA. Or 'From liberated fashions to fashionable liberations'?

JANE. Meeow!

SPORTS PAGES

DOMINIC *visiting*.

DOMINIC. If you want me to cover your championships it'll cost you high in expenses. I'll spice it with the obligatory champagne-and-strawberries atmosphere, you pay for it.

RONNIE. You'll get what my budget will allow.

DOMINIC. A most miserly attitude if I may say so, and one not worthy of your race. Why, after all, should you not give something extra for those talented such as myself, who have something extra to offer?

MARVIN. You're not the *most* brilliant tennis reporter we have.

DOMINIC. Oh I am, I am. And you know that I am.

MARVIN. Besides, your expenses come from Business News.

DOMINIC. It's true. I can't lie. My expenses are the highest on the *Sunday Paper* on account of the terrible, terrible amount of bribing I have to do among trade union officials.

RONNIE. You're a cynical man, Dominic.

DOMINIC. Cynical I am not. Spoilt, perhaps. But then we can't all have interesting backgrounds like you, Ronnie. Russian Jewish immigrants from the East End of London? Were you really born in the East End? God! How I resent my father for being so rich. All the best people were born in a ghetto. If only my father had bought *us* a ghetto, one we could go to for weekends. Now that would have been something.

IN DEPTH

PAT. Well, someone on your sodding paper ought to be interested.

CHRIS. I've tried, love, honest I have.

PAT. I mean, it's more than just another abortion story, it's a story about your knotty medical problems and your callous authority.

CHRIS. That's what I said: 'Knotty medical problems and callous authority,' I said. Try it on Mary. She's got Pete's job for this month.

ARTS PAGES

ERNST. I can't review this book. I find his writing so awful and I gave his last one such a knocking that I'm beginning to feel it's unfair. Gives me guilts. No reviewer should have to feel guilty.

SEBASTIAN. Especially if he's also a novelist!

SPORTS PAGES

MARVIN. So there I was, in Northern Ireland, soldiers shot at, civilians murdered, bombs going off everywhere, reporting on a game of golf. Jesus! I thought, what the hell am I doing covering a game of golf?

BUSINESS NEWS

The FINK *is introducing himself to* MORTY.

MORTY *(shaking hands)*. And you're the gentleman with information on Onyx Foods?

FINK *(patting his briefcase)*. Minute research. It's all here. I take it I can speak openly? Good. The basis of my information is this: that Lesley Crafton — Crafty Crafton I call him — has stated a share price since 1967 based on a false market, and that he's been able to achieve this through a complicated system of interlocking holdings which work roughly in this way: the English company takes over a French company which is then able to buy shares in the subsidiary of the English company which then buys shares in a subsidiary of the French company and so on. Clever? Ah, very clever is our Crafty Crafton. Now, look at these graphs of share price rises and rising profits ...

ARTS PAGES

SEBASTIAN. Oh, my God! Another poem. We always get them after disasters or Prince Philip's birthday. Says a great deal for the soul of the British public, I suppose, but doesn't contribute much to British poetry.

EDITOR'S OFFICE

Editorial continuing.

HARVEY. What's your centre piece this week?

GORDON. A finely argued piece of demolition on the myth of the silent majority which makes the very simple but devastating point that the convenience of such a concept as silence is — the silence.

HARVEY. Quite right! If you say nothing anybody can claim to speak for you. Lovely! Splendid! And the leaders? Anthony? How about one on the Persian Gulf?

ANTHONY. Do you want it to have a message? A punch line?

HARVEY. Yes, start with that joke about the Arabs.

ANTHONY. Which one?

HARVEY. Oh, that one about — how does it go? You know, showing how they can't ever agree on anything.

BUSINESS NEWS

The FINK's story, continuing.

FINK. Now, I'd been following him so closely that I understood the pattern of Crafty Crafton's behaviour, his psychology as it were, and of course, when his shares were at 71 I bought them because I knew, from watching his dealings, that they'd soon go up to 93 or thereabouts, which they did, and at which point I sold. And who's the Mafia, as it were, in all this? Snuff! Oh don't laugh. *(Dips into his briefcase for large foreign magazines.)* Snuff is the new narcotic. You can put your L.S.D. into it. Kids in Germany and Sweden are doing it all the time. And so Mr Crafty Crafton and his Jewish backers are putting their money into snuff. Large profits, you see. Now, that's not all ...

WOMEN'S PAGES

ANGELA. Oh yes, I agree, the elegant sneer is always admired. And if it's like Pope it's very good indeed.

JANE. Problem is, it's rarely like Pope.

BUSINESS NEWS

The FINK'*s story, continuing.*

FINK. So, you're asking, where is all this leading? His saga seems endless and many vaulted, you're thinking to yourself. Nearly there. I've told you about Crafton's dealings on the Continent and at home. I've told you his motives and about the habit of his Jewish brethren in helping poorer members or their community. So, we know, they stick together. And my final proof of this is from an old friend who sees these same brethren — Morgenstein the banker and Rosenthals of Town and Country Investments, big men, the biggest, you agree? The biggest! Always in company with Crafton. Three of them, always together. In golf clubs, restaurants, everywhere, my friend sees them — now why?

D

ARTS PAGES

ERNST. Yes, I do! I do think writing novels is more difficult than writing plays. A play is just dialogue confined to a physical space. Its canvas *can't* be large. A novel demands more attention to detail, greater psychological exploration, a richer grasp of plot. Its space and movement is unlimited and you've only yourself to rely on. No actors to fill out thinly drawn characters, no director to give rhythms which the material doesn't contain, and no lighting man playing tricks in order to create moods which the plot can't substantiate.

SEBASTIAN. Are you suggesting D. H. Lawrence is greater than Shakespeare?

ERNST. No, but I *am* suggesting Shakespeare's not as great as Tolstoy.

BUSINESS NEWS

The FINK, *who has gradually become excited by his own story, allows his enthusiasm to take over from his judgment.*

FINK. I'll be honest, lay my cards on the table. I'm obsessed by the European Jewish Mafia. Been reading about them as far back as the time Napoleon freed the Jews. And here's my point, think about it. There's the tightly knit Jewish families of Rothschilds, Mannerheims, and Herzens on the Continent, and Messrs Morgenstein, Rosenthal and Crafton in this country. And now *(Clasps his fingers together.)* with the

European Common Market — click! The opportunity they've been waiting for — a highly closed plot in the traditional Jewish manner trying to dominate the important areas of food and leisure. *(Pause)* You must not, however, think I'm anti-semitic.

POLITICAL AND FEATURES

MARY. Shall I tell you what's wrong with your article on futurology?

NORMAN. I'd prefer you not to.

MARY. You believe them.

NORMAN. That's not true.

MARY. You ask a very reasonable question: Has technology rearranged the genes of political issues? And then you give *their* answer: yes, it has!

NORMAN. I happen to agree with them.

MARY. Have you ever asked yourself why their books are so thick?

NORMAN. Scholarship.

MARY. Balls! It's because they have to make so many allowances and qualifications for their predictions. The very size of their books contradicts their claims for accurate forecast.

NORMAN. They don't claim accuracy, just high probability.

MARY. If men were robots you'd need only a little book of graphs. But they're not. They're human, unpredictable, millions of individual wills, all different — hence, a large book of hedged bets.

(HARRY enters.)

Any luck?

HARRY. To be honest I changed tactics.

MARY. Meaning?

HARRY. I went to Llantrisant, where the strike was. Thought I'd get more of a lead there.

NORMAN. Do you know I was evacuated to Llantrisant?

MARY. So, if your secret society did plan to contact the Angries you've missed them. And we don't even know if they exist.

HARRY *(handing her a sheet)*. I think I've got evidence to prove that. I picked up this roneoed document which was in the latest strike pay packet. A sort of manifesto. Very flowery stuff. Not like the Angries at all. Correct grammar and statements with some degree of lucidity, except the end, which—

MARY *(who's been reading it)*. Eureka! Harry, keep on to that Angries cell. It may lead to something fantastic. Fan-tastic! 'Scuse me. *(She rushes out.)*

WOMEN'S PAGES

JANE. It's a terrible confession—but my colleagues depress me. They play this great game at work and then they shuffle home on the commuter train to suburbia.

ANGELA. Well, thank God for the fantasy world, I say. Compensates for lilliputian lives.

JANE. That's what we are. Lilliputians! Always wanting to bring down giants.

ANGELA. I seem to spend my time building them.

JANE. *They* are paper giants. But the real ones—we never celebrate the real ones.

ANGELA. Oh, I don't know. Business News celebrate Arnold Weinstock. Arts Pages celebrate Hughie Green.

JANE. Fashions! Novelty! We celebrate fashions and novelties.

ANGELA. And *you're* beginning to depress *me*.

JANE. Well, do something about it.

ARTS PAGES

ERNST. And shall I tell you why I *don't* go to the theatre? It's pampered. There's more paraphernalia attached to a first night than the appearance of a novel.

JOHN. Ah ha! Now we have it.

ERNST. Isn't it true? And there's *no* fuss at all about the appearance of a play on television and *that's* a medium enjoyed by millions!

JOHN. Demagogue!

EDITOR'S OFFICE

MARY *visiting*.

HARVEY *(who's been reading* HARRY's *document)*. It's slim, Mary.

MARY. The *exact* words, though. 'The patterns men can make for the pleasure of their living.' The same awful words. Morgan King! The man himself. Behind all those boyish Robin Hood antics.

HARVEY. Maybe they're not his words. Maybe I made a mistake and he was quoting from a poem or a Hazlitt essay or something, and he and this group — whoever they are — were using the same source, coincidentally. Have a look, Gordon.

MARY. Coincidentally! Bloody strange coincidence. Harvey,

Morgan King has formed a secret society of political Robin Hoods. I *know* it. It all fits in with his shifty passions. One of my sons attended a series of seminars he gave at Oxford and from the way he describes him he sounds quite capable of seducing a small band of over-heated romantic imaginations into playing Tupamaros.

GORDON. Not good enough, Mary. I'd say you needed more evidence.

MARY. I think you're all frightened.

HARVEY. No, cautious.

MARY. So am I. I'm not asking us to print anything, but it's worth following up, for God's sake.

HARVEY. You're relentless.

MARY. So you keep saying. Hell! I can see I won't get much joy here. *(She leaves.)*

FOREIGN DEPT.

MORTY *visiting.*

MORTY. And suddenly I realise. This Fink's spinning me the old yarn about the Jewish conspiracy to take over the world. Poor bloody Jews. Can't do anything right, can we? Jesus, Marx, Freud, Trotsky, you, me – all part of some conspiracy or other. So I tell him about this Scotsman: 65, lives in Switzerland, the only man I know who can reach into his back pocket and produce enough cash to buy a company. Started off by imagining he could make his fortune out of surgical machinery, but he did what few others bother to do – he actually took the trouble to get himself qualified as a surgeon in order to test whether his inventions worked.

Strange man. Hates unions. A sort of élitist fascist, but not wholly without charm. Anyway ...

EDITOR'S OFFICE

ANGELA *visiting.*

ANGELA. Well, we're staking pretty big claims as the most serious paper in the country.

HARVEY. And it's true.

ANGELA. Then let me bring the Women's Pages into the science-versus-politics issue.

HARVEY. What are you thinking of?

ANGELA. Oh, I don't know. Are women more attracted to science than politics and is there a reason? That sort of thing.

GORDON. You think women aspire to the practical rather than the empirical?

ANGELA. Could be. We just want the go ahead in principle.

HARVEY. You've got it, you've got it.

ANGELA. Hallelujah!

POLITICAL AND FEATURES

TAMARA *visiting.* NORMAN *has been reading the proofs of her latest piece.*

NORMAN *(handing it back).* It's reasonable, Tamara, reasonable.

TAMARA. That's a good word. Norman. Succinct and diminishing. Thank you.

NORMAN. Now don't sulk.

TAMARA. Oh, how I'd just like to slide around, with no purpose, having little conversations.

NORMAN. Only you can't quite give up the glamour of catching a plane and having access to important people.

TAMARA. Can't I?

CYNTHIA. None of us can.

TAMARA. *Important* people? My contempt for the Western European politicians I've had to meet is gradually extending to the whole spectrum of human beings — important or not.

NEWS ROOM

MARY *visiting, with* PAT *at her heels.*

MARY *(to* PAUL*).* Paul, who the hell turned this away?

PAUL. It's only another abortion story.

MARY. Another abortion story? Another *abortion* story?

PAUL. I can turn you up ten stories about girls of thirteen, twelve, eleven, even ten having abortions.

MARY. That's why I have to go through everything myself.

PAUL. Look, Mary, as News editor *I* judge the kind of news story we should be printing.

MARY. Judge? You couldn't judge between a Neasden beauty competition and a Middle East war.

PAUL. It came up in the editorial, why didn't you talk then?

MARY. I wasn't there.

PAUL. Well, that's hardly my fault.

MARY *(storming off).* I want this woman hung, drawn and quartered. She's a National Health Service gynaecologist and

she's not paid with my money to offer moral judgments to
12-year-old girls in need of help ...

PAT. Thanks!

POLITICAL AND FEATURES

NORMAN. Well, I'm sorry — it *is* just a reasonable article because
it *is* rather difficult to generate excitement about obscure
Indian tribes in Latin America. I mean it may look good in
print when you read a D. H. Lawrence novel, but Quetzal-
coatl *does* sound funny when you actually have to *say* it.

TAMARA. Oh, your bloody English upper-class wit! You can't
look anybody in the face without your Empire but you still
go on making pale jokes about the funny names of aliens.
Haven't you heard that no one finds you funny any longer
except your pudding-faced working-class? They can always
be relied upon to find the sound of Vladivostok good for a
giggle.

CYNTHIA. Norman's hardly working-class.

TAMARA. What difference? Both classes waddle with smugness,
like dogs and their owners.

CYNTHIA. True, true. We've lived with each other for so long
you know, we do rather look alike.

TAMARA. And you'll never change, never! Your ruling-class
is so good mannered in gratitude for its privileges and your
worker so brain-washed with kindness that he does everything his master does.

NORMAN. What's wrong with kindness, pray? Is every honest
virtue now a form of insult?

TAMARA. Kindness as a right! But not as a payment. 'Leave me
my privileges and I'll be kind to you. Honour the privacy of

my mansion, I'll honour the privacy of your backyard'. And so of course he'll mouth his master's prejudice against foreigners — a small price to pay for a pat on the head.

IN DEPTH

MARY *rushes in followed by a bemused* PAT.

MARY. Right! Drop your bridges.

CHRIS. Did she say 'drop your breeches'?

MARY. I want this gynaecologist investigated.

JULIAN. Hell, Mary, it's a news story not an In Depth exposé.

MARY. It's more important than a news story. The mother herself has asked us to investigate. Problem is the doctor's clammed up. Refuses to speak to the press.

JULIAN. I don't blame her.

MARY. What we want is the story of a guilty gynaecologist. Was she married? Did she have an unhappy love affair, broken marriage? Are there any children?

CHRIS. That's Harold Robbins, not journalism.

MARY. And get a photograph, even if it's of her peering reluctantly round a door.

JULIAN. A classic News Room story.

MARY. Pat, get this photostated.

PAT. How many?

MARY. About 10. Julian, you can get up there in two and a half hours on the M.1.

JULIAN. Three.

CHRIS. Four.

JULIAN. And basically what you want is all the dirt I can get on her?

MARY. Yes. And get photographs of the girl and her mother. Door-step them if necessary.

JULIAN. How can you take a moral position about the gynae-cologist if you start invading people's privacy?

MARY. I'll worry about that. *(She leaves.)*

JULIAN. It's too late. We go to press in twenty-four hours. Bloody News Room should've handled it.

CHRIS. If we're getting other people's chestnuts out of the fire that's tough, but that's what we're paid for.

WOMEN'S PAGES

ANGELA *(entering)*. We're in business.

JANE. He agreed?

ANGELA. Of course he agreed. I don't know why we didn't push earlier.

JANE. Do you think the story of Lysistrata comes under the heading of science versus politics?

ANGELA. That's sex versus politics.

JANE. But the Greek girls didn't have contraception—and that's science.

ANGELA. So?

JANE. Well, the general's ladies could last out longer today by safely taking their favours elsewhere.

ANGELA. Bit of a strain on the imagination, that.

FOREIGN DEPT.

GORDON. Now, this is what I mean about religious dogma leading to massacres. *(Reading from* The Times.*)* ' "My dear

countrymen, peace be with you," he said in his speech
announcing war. "Our enemy has again challenged us. The
Indian armed forces have launched wanton attacks on
Pakistan on several fronts. India's dislike and enmity of
Pakistan is well-known the world over. It has always been its
endeavour to weaken Pakistan and destroy it. This fresh and
grave aggression on the part of India is the greatest and last
move against us. We have shown great forbearance but the
time has now come when we must give the enemy a most
effective answer. One hundred and twenty million crusaders
of Pakistan, you have the support and blessings of Allah."'

TAMARA. Uch! Vain! Pompous! Demagogues! How I despise
them.

EDITOR'S OFFICE

Editorial continuing.

ANTHONY. Has the Chancellor read the typescript of his interview with Mary?

HARVEY. Not yet. Why?

ANTHONY. I hardly think he's going to approve of all her witty
little interjections. ' "It is a cruel statement to make," the
Chancellor continued, "but men are dustmen or lavatory
attendants or machine minders or policemen because of
intellectual limitations." I resisted the temptation to ask if
he had statistics on how many intellectually limited sons of
the upper classes became dustmen.'

HARVEY. Heavy-handed but he does need knocking.

ANTHONY. Well, why didn't she simply make the point to him
and get his reply?

HARVEY. Nor is the Commissioner of Police going to be happy to have his force labelled 'intellectually limited'.

BUSINESS NEWS

MORTY (to someone off-stage). Yes, well, I believe in the capitalist system so I have no conflicts. Conflicts? Hah! I've been looking for them for years. Always wanted to be able to resign on a matter of principle.

FOREIGN DEPT.

GORDON (still reading from The Times). ' "Your land is filled with the love of the Holy Prophet. The enemy has once again challenged our will." '
TAMARA. I just don't believe it.
GORDON. ' "Rise as one for your honour and stand like an impregnable wall of steel in the face of your enemy." '
TAMARA. And on and on and on …

POLITICAL AND FEATURES

MARY. I think I'm tired.
CYNTHIA. You think so? You're not sure?
MARY. And I've got my mother for dinner tonight. She's never tired.
CYNTHIA. Menopause?

MARY. No. Never worried me. I waited and waited, dreading all those horror stories—but it came and went, nothing! Except backache and other trivial reminders of creeping old age.

CYNTHIA. Don't you ever think of peppering evenings with mum?

MARY. Oh, Jason'll be there.

CYNTHIA. Your ex-husband seems to be the only man you ever see these days.

MARY. Only really intelligent man I know. Bloody fierce intelligence he's got. Puts our youngsters in their place whenever they come out with such things as (Mockingly) 'Intelligence isn't everything, you know!' God knows why I agreed to divorce him.

CYNTHIA. Why did you?

MARY. Used each other up. Why else? Some couples accept it, others don't. Simple.

CYNTHIA. Oh, very.

FOREIGN DEPT.

GORDON (still reading from The Times). ' "You have right and justice on your side." '

TAMARA. Always!

GORDON. ' "Pounce on the enemy in a spirit of confidence and let the enemy know that every Pakistani is determined to stand up for the defence of the dear motherland." '

TAMARA. No one ever learns.

GORDON. ' "The brave soldiers of our army have shown unparalleled bravery and stopped the advance of the enemy." '

TAMARA. As though history never happens for them.

BUSINESS NEWS

MORTY (*to someone off-stage*). And what's more, Arnold Weinstock is one of the most intelligent men we've met who's
more intelligent than us, and we don't meet many of them!

FOREIGN DEPT.

GORDON (*still reading from* The Times). ' "The enemy knows
that victory in war does not go to those who have numerical
strength and large quantities of military hardware. It goes to
those who have faith in their mission and in the ideals of
Islam and who believe God helps the righteous." '

TAMARA. And who will help us? Dear God, who will help the
rest of us?

PART FOUR

THE CENTRE SPACE

A table in a restaurant.
MARY *is dining with* OLIVER MASSINGHAM, *Under-Secretary of
State for Foreign and Commonwealth Affairs.*
They are friends.
She is slightly drunk.

MASSINGHAM. I hope you're not disappointed, Mary. Lumbered

with a mere under-secretary rather than the Foreign Minister himself?

MARY. You think I'm drunk for that reason, Oliver?

MASSINGHAM. He hates interviews. All that personality cultify-ing.

MARY. Who does he think — no! I mustn't.

MASSINGHAM. Mustn't what?

MARY. I've been told by my children that my only contribution to British journalism is to have elevated the gutter question 'Who does he think he is?' to a respected art form.

MASSINGHAM. And that hurt, of course.

MARY. It *should* have hurt. Everything should hurt. But nothing does. Oliver — this is off the record, but here's a question I've been dying to ask one of you only I didn't dare. Your wife, I know the situation, this dinner, she'll give you hell. No, no. We're old friends. Don't protest. My question. It goes like this: you're a minister. I've watched the House in action: fights, battles of wit, and intellect — but, that's not all, is it? Thems not the only battles, is they? There's personality conflicts also — in the cabinet, in ministerial departments, with cantankerous old civil servants. And then — tact! Diplomacy! Different kinds, in different ways, to different people. The public face on the one hand and the private re-assurance to industry, the unions, the foreign ambassadors on the other. A great juggling act, wits alert all the time. To say nothing of all you're supposed to know about the nation's affairs *outside* your particular department. And on top of all this, on *top* — of all *this*, there's the problems of being a husband, a lover, a father, a friend, uncle, brother — God wot! *(Pause)* How-do-you-do-it-for-God's-sake? How? How don't you become overwhelmed by it all? Do certain arteries harden? Is part of you callous? Like the doctor, or the writer? Tell me.

MASSINGHAM. Mary, I think you're very drunk.

MARY. But still functioning, eh? My lovely brain still ticking — tick-tick-tick-tick.

MASSINGHAM. Perhaps I should take advantage of your lovely, drunk brain and get you to talk about yourself for a change.

MARY. Me? Oh, I had a famous father, didn't you know? Famous for what they called in his day 'thought-provoking' novels. Only his fame was media-made and his thoughts provoked very few, very shallowly, and his day didn't last long. I used to taunt him in front of my university friends about having nothing to say to my generation and he used to take notice and rush to read my required reading. I had to grow up in the growing darkness of his demission and watch his lively pleasure, at being recognised in the streets, change into a grey anonymity. He was a gentle man, made for the comforts fame brings and which the Gods gave him only a tantalising taste of. And I, with innocent devastation, went into competition with him. I won, of course. Because good fathers never let their children lose. He stepped back, graciously, for the sake of a healthy family, following the false principle, which many half-baked artists follow, that if he couldn't create a healthy, happy family he couldn't create a worthy work of literature. He created nothing from that moment on. Defeated! And I understood none of that.

NEWS ROOM

It's a Saturday.
The still slide of the printing presses now becomes a film of men preparing the machines ready for use.

The paper is being laid out. Mainly the front page. Movement is reaching towards a height.
(This area can now be filled with actors who've played other parts.)
HARVEY *is standing beside a man who's sitting drawing possible layouts on a blank sheet.*

HARVEY. Right, we'll have the Indo-Pakistan war on the left, conductor and his baby centre space, cholera here and map over the top, here, and that leaves this area for the gynaecologist story, if there is one. Mary? Where's Mary?

NORMAN. Having a cool argument with the In Depth boys.

ANTHONY. Will someone tell me why we're featuring a photograph on the front page of a 51-year-old opera conductor with his 18-month-old baby in his arms?

NORMAN. Well, we've got a story about an outbreak of another little bloody war, one about the spread of cholera, a morbid piece about a mother urging her daughter to death in order to save her from the shame of producing a bastard and so, with a gruesome front page like that, don't you think we need a drop of human warmth? To make our millions of readers like the world just a little bit better on their Sunday off work?

ANTHONY. May I remind you, Harvey, that our messengers are still on strike and copy's not moving?

HARVEY. Ronnie's with Mac now.

SPORTS PAGES

MAC. Pensions are rotten in this place, Ronnie, and you know it.

RONNIE. I know it, but —

MAC. And I'm not advising my men back until management

agree to postpone the date for cancelling closure of the garage so we have time to discuss them.

RONNIE. Look, Mac. Sometimes, I've got to say it, and I can as one union official to another, sometimes you boys cut off your nose to spite your face. I'd never say that to management, but between you and me that's what I think.

MAC. That's not friendly, Ronnie.

RONNIE. Friendly? Do you know that your boys stopped the Securicor van from bringing in the cash the other day? Now who do you think that affects? Not us, or management. We all get paid monthly, by cheque, straight into our banks. No! The office girls. The poor bloody office girls. We had to whip round in this office and pay the secretary.

MAC. All wars have their innocent casualties.

RONNIE. Cant! Don't give me cant, Mac. Look, time's pressing. Release your messengers, get copy flowing again so's we can get the paper out and I promise you I'll persuade our chapel to give two weeks' notice of strike if no agreement is reached on redundancies. Agreed?

MAC. Can you guarantee it?

RONNIE. Come on, Mac. You know I can't *guarantee* a thing like that. Agreed?

MAC. If it doesn't work, Ronnie, I promise you, we'll get the whole of Fleet Street out and no one, anywhere, will have a paper.

(MAC *leaves.* RONNIE *has been dialling meanwhile.*)

RONNIE (*into phone*). We've got a newspaper!

NEWS ROOM

SECRETARY (*Yelling to* HARVEY). We've got a newspaper!

HARVEY. Great! Mary, where's Mary?

(MARY *appears with copy.*)

MARY. Alright, I agree, it *is* a news story. As long as she goes on the front page I don't mind.

HARVEY. And the bridges story'll go into In Depth where it belongs. Good. Got a photograph?

MARY. Messengers should've brought one from the dark-room.

HARVEY. The first interviews read splendidly, by the way.

MARY. Thanks, but don't patronise me, Harvey.

HARVEY. Cheer up, Mary. We nearly didn't have a paper this week.

(MESSENGER *arrives with photo.*)

My God! She looks so hounded.

MARY. It'll be a lesson to other moralising gynaecologists. *She* hounded that poor child. *(She leaves.)*

SPORTS PAGES

MARVIN *(on phone)*. But, Ned, we haven't got the space. We've already had to cut down on the swimming championships — it's a small paper this week. Wait, that's not a decision I can make, I'll ask Ronnie. Ronnie, Ned reporting the Arsenal-West Ham match, he says the Hammers' new player is the greatest genius in the history of football.

RONNIE. That's because he's a university graduate with a first-class arts degree and Ned's a snob. What does he want?

MARVIN. Another 300 words.

RONNIE. No doubt it'll be full of poetry about the geometry of the game but tell him 150. It'll have to go into six-point.

NEWS ROOM

The following snatches of conversation fly back and forth among the miscellaneous characters who flood this area.

SECRETARY *(clutching phone)*. Our copy taker is in chaos and Ian is sitting in his hotel waiting to dictate — can anyone do something about it?

SOMEONE. Right! We're going to that wedding after all. It's royalty and the chief feels a little responsible *to* them or *for* them or *something* ...

SOMEONE. It *was* a good story until the subs got at it — inky-fingered bloody maniacs ...

HARVEY *(to SOMEONE)*. Ring him up, tell him copy is O.K. but ask him what he means by the top of page 7 where it says 'the secret transcripts have been released!' *What* transcripts have been released, by whom, to whom and about what ...

PAUL *(to HARVEY)*. Harvey, first edition of the *People*, look. They've got an exclusive on the Prime Minister's private earnings.

HARVEY. Damn! We got anybody on to it?

PAUL. No one free.

HARVEY. I'll do it myself.

LAYOUT. Where you thinking of putting it, Harvey?

HARVEY. That's the problem.

ANTHONY. Do you really think it's that important?

HARVEY. What, after we published his diary extracts? We'd be laughed at to miss this. Right! We'll take the cholera map out and cut the last quarter column.

LAYOUT. And put the money story where?

HARVEY. Bit at the top here, across five columns, over the Indian headline.

ANTHONY. Then we won't be the 'only one going to town on the cholera epidemic'.

HARVEY. Not the moment to be facetious, Anthony.

POLITICAL AND FEATURES

MESSENGER *comes in with a letter.*

MESSENGER. Letter for Miss Mortimer.
    (*She reads a few lines.*)

MARY. Jesus Christ! (*She moves quickly to the door to call the* MESSENGER *back.*) What did he look like?

MESSENGER. Who, miss?

MARY. The man who gave you this letter, describe him, quick.

MESSENGER. Well, I don't know, do I? Reception give it to me and I just give it to you, didn't I?
    (*He leaves.* MARY *whips up phone, dials. It's picked up in the News Room.*)

MARY. Harvey, please.

SECRETARY. For you, Harvey.

MARY. Harvey? Can I see you? Alone?

HARVEY. I'm just about to start on the P.M.'s earnings. What is it?

MARY. Something on Morgan King. I've *got* to see you.

HARVEY. Well, briefly then, in my office.
    (MARY *is about to rush out.*)

CYNTHIA. What's all that, then?

MARY. Morgan King and kidnappings. Tell you later. (*She leaves.*)

BUSINESS NEWS

DOMINIC *(he's slightly drunk)*. Women! Ah, women! I love them! I mean there was this girl in Cornwall, in a pub, with a skirt just above her pubic hairs, indifferent to hostility, sublime in her sensuousness, with thighs! Ah! those thighs. Thighs which alone you'd want to spend three hours licking. And Christ! I knew the way straight through to her and she knew I knew. And when I think about it I could weep! Weep! Every time! To think it could happen to *me*. Their touch, their look, their smells. I *love* a woman who smells of action. When she works in a garage there's a smell of oil lingering around her. If she's a doctor — it's medicinal. A painter — the smell of paints. I love the smell of alcohol on her breath when she drinks; of her body after she runs. Anything that tells me she moves, is alive with decisions, agitated. Fuck your art! Fuck your politics! Fuck your conversation! Even your wine. Women! I can't bear to be without them.

EDITOR'S OFFICE

HARVEY *has just finished reading the letter* MARY's *handed him.*

MARY. What do you think?

HARVEY. It's suspect.

MARY. Not to me it isn't.

HARVEY. And we'll end up with the biggest libel suit in the history of Fleet Street.

MARY. Here's what I suggest. We've got three hours till the last edition. Can the bridges hold over till next week?

HARVEY. Till eternity, I should think.

MARY. This man's waiting for me across the road in the pub. I'll take Chris and see what he's got to say. If the documents he's got look authentic then we'll reproduce them and just ask questions. No comment.

HARVEY. They'll have to be bloody authentic. Can we get hold of a sample of his handwriting to check?

MARY. I've got someone doing that already. We'll spend an hour with the fink, an hour to write it and it can be on the stone in good time for the last press as an In Depth story.

HARVEY. You're rushing, Mary.

MARY. I *know*, I just know in my bones — these documents will be conclusive. I've pursued this man for a year now, Harvey, and I've warned — he's a phoney of the most offensive sort and it's our responsibility to —

HARVEY. Mary, have you thought, that if he's linked with the robbing of supermarkets for old-age pensioners, bank robberies to pay strikers, kidnapping managers to give them lessons in civility, then you'll do just what you don't want, you'll make him a martyr.

MARY. Nonsense! The English temperament can't stand martyrs.

HARVEY. Maybe. But you'll do well to remember that this nation was weaned on the myths of King Arthur, a holy grail and the merry men of Sherwood Forest.

MARY. He'll be none of those things by the time I've finished with him.

HARVEY. And there's another thing. I've got a sneaking admiration for the enterprise. It appeals to me.

MARY. Well, it doesn't to me. It's the wrong tone of voice. Half-baked revolutionaries who've borrowed other people's tongues. Do you really see urban guerrillas operating in

Clapham Common? The Morgan Kings of this world are ashamed of their minds like the Victorians were ashamed of their bodies, so they flirt with revolution in a pathetic attempt to be men of action. It irritates me. Wastes energy. Misleads real fervour, real enthusiasm, real protest. It's sentimental nonsense which belongs neither to our nature, our history or our situation and I despise it.

HARVEY. Mary, some advice.

MARY. Not now, Harvey.

HARVEY. Yes, *just* now. Remember this: a journalist is only engaged in handing on fragments of information. You can spice it with comment but don't fall into the trap of exaggerated pronouncements.

MARY. Harvey, I don't think —

HARVEY. Well, I *do* think. You can't reveal, you can only inform. Don't simplify what's complex and then imagine you've clarified the truth. And it *is* complex, it's frighteningly complex. New states being born, new classes, races finding their voice, feeling their strengths. A time ripe for opportunists who can mouth the platitudes of pain and suffering, and incite the sweet taste of revenge. Anything can happen: a glorious release of all that's noble in men or a murderous unleashing of savage spites and envies. And we have the power to tip it one way or the other; not simply by what we say but *the way we say it*. The habit of knocking down gods is very seductive and contagious and we're very good at being spiteful. I'm not all that proud of the history of journalism, Mary, but I don't want to see the *Sunday Paper* perpetuating it.

MARY. But why *this* — to *me* — *now*?

HARVEY. Because each 'god' you topple chips away at your own self-respect. The damage you do to others can boomerang and destroy you. That's why.

MARY. The duty of this paper, since we're handing out advice, is to investigate secret and well-protected misbehaviour – of any kind.

HARVEY. I don't need to be told that. Nor should I need to point out that there's no institution more 'well protected' than a newspaper.

MARY. This is silly. What are we shouting at each other for? Look, Harvey, I believe passionately that there's no other country where the administration of society is carried out more honestly, humanely and conscientiously than here. But that doesn't mean we've got a society so perfect that we can afford to limit democratic scrutiny.

HARVEY. I'm simply warning you. You might want to deflate the egos of self-styled 'gods' but be careful you don't crack the confidence of good men. We haven't got that many. Think of it.

MARY. I don't really think I needed all that. (*She leaves.*)

POLITICAL AND FEATURES

NORMAN. She's lucky, Mary. She can insult fools. Not me. I'm damned to suffer their offensive company for ever because I can see that while the stupid man pours out his stupidity – he knows it. And I can't return the offence of showing that *I* know it. Embarrasses me. Perhaps that's why I'm a journalist, there's distance between the insult and the insulted.

ARTS PAGES

ERNST. Ever thought of asking a critic 'not to bother this week'?

JOHN. What, him give up his precious space?

SEBASTIAN. My dear fellow, people opening their Sunday paper look forward to reading a critic's piece. Wouldn't miss it for the world. Even if it is only a bumbling on.

JOHN. Funny creatures, critics.

ERNST. Are they any good at taking criticism of their criticism?

SEBASTIAN. Most accommodating. The better they are the less they mind what you say. It's only the minor critics who go into tantrums.

IN DEPTH

MARY *visiting.*

MARY. Chris, take a break and come and have a drink with a fink.

CHRIS. A gentle fink or an evil fink? My nerves are feeling frayed.

MARY. A Morgan King fink.

JULIAN. Ah! A king-sized fink.

CHRIS. Gossip or documents?

MARY. You know I never listen to gossip. Hurry, if it looks good I want to catch the last edition.

CHRIS. St George moves in for the kill.

MARY. Alright, alright! He's misunderstood. *I'm* the dragon. Shall we move?

CHRIS. I fly, I fly. Watch me how I fly.

(*They leave.*)

POLITICAL AND FEATURES

CYNTHIA. I once knew a beautiful young boy who was like that.

Everyone wanted to embrace him, me for example. And he was so sensitive to the embarrassment of refusal that he let me. Men, women — they all wanted to touch him. The more brazen seduced him outright — some people have a nose for these things, they can smell out victims. That's what he was, a victim. And so gradually he began avoiding people, shunned all contacts, withdrew. At the age of thirty he was consigned to a home, morose, confused. Born for abuse.

FOREIGN DEPT.

The urgent sound of 'tick-tack'.
GORDON *and* TAMARA *standing by the telex.*

GORDON *(reading)*. 'At least 250 doctors, professors, writers and teachers, the cream of the intellectuals who could have helped create the state of Bangladesh, were found murdered in a field outside Dacca.'
    (TAMARA turns away.)
'All had their hands tied behind their backs and had been bayoneted, garotted or shot.' Tamara, get this down to Harvey. It's Reuter's, everyone'll have it. Tamara!

TAMARA. I —

GORDON. For Christ's sake, you're a journalist. Is this any worse than your reports on the Eichman trial?

TAMARA. *You* see it as a bestial but inevitable tactic, don't you? It makes a morbid sense to take away your enemy's intellectual cream, doesn't it?

GORDON. It's war.

TAMARA. It's more. That bit of slaughter? It's a signpost. In that **single** act there's such — such darkness. You know what it is? It's the poisonous side of the sweet apple of democracy. It's Mary's 'who-does-he-think-he-is?' gone insane. It's what your lovely, ordinary everyman would like to do in order to feel equal—massacre the thinkers.

GORDON. Don't be a bloody fool. Men have been slaughtering their thinkers for centuries.

TAMARA. How blithely you say it.

NEWS ROOM

SECRETARY (*on phone*). Time Life? Paul Mannering's secretary here. Yes, the same one. We can't afford two and I cost too much. It's about that article he promised you—it's my fault that it's not arrived. I forgot to give him your message about the new date-line. Will tomorrow do? Thanks. 'Bye. Holy mother of God forgive me for my sins.

MARTIN. How much are they paying you for all that, Kathy?

SECRETARY. Well, they get a separate bill for every lie I tell—if that's what you mean.

FOREIGN DEPT.

TAMARA. I don't think I can really cope much more, Gordon.

GORDON. Go home. I'll finish your story.

TAMARA. Between the oppressors and the fanatics there's the rest of us.

GORDON. Go to a cinema, or the opera.

TAMARA. Helpless.

GORDON. Spoil yourself. Buy yourself a present—records, a dress.

TAMARA. We're always so helpless.

GORDON. Or what about those antique markets you love so much. Take a stroll down Portobello.

TAMARA. Uch! Depressing! They never used to—but now antique markets depress me. Bits and pieces of cups and saucers at exorbitant prices. Cracked plates, torn lace, threadbare shawls, frail discarded toys. Old ladies' homes bought for a few pence and sold at such a profit, such a terrible profit. And all done in the sweet tones of a dear friend advising you, flattering your taste, challenging your courage to spend by saying this or that's too expensive for you. All fraudulent, cheating, such charming conmanship—and insulting. Above all insulting, and offensive, and greedy, and insulting and greedy, greedy, greedy!

BUSINESS NEWS

JANE *approaching* DOMINIC *with a bottle of whisky.*

JANE. With the compliments of Women's Pages.

MORTY. And what's he done that we haven't?

DOMINIC. Gave the girls a little anecdote about the man who was refused sterilization on the National Health.

MORTY. You selling your life story again?

DOMINIC. Oh, very funny. But I tell you the population explosion is serious. I can hardly park my car for people in the way.

SPORTS PAGES

RONNIE. I mean it's like a marriage conflict, isn't it? All social conflict is like marital conflict in that only a minor incident is needed to revive the bitterness of past abuse. That's what this strike was really about. I mean what's the sacking of thirty men, comparatively? Enough of a problem, of course. But as it goes on it becomes magnified by the recollection of old enmities 'and thus the native hue of resolution is sicklied o'er with the pale cast of thought' and we're clogged by irrelevant but all too vivid memories. Do you think that when a union leader sits facing an employer he's merely confronting a man who wants to pay him less than he's asking? Never! He's confronting a personality to whom he needs to show how he too can argue, be firm, tough, wield power. Have you ever seen the conference rooms in trade union offices? Replicas of city board rooms. What you might call 'Jewish baronialism'. And when he confronts a really aristocratic employer it's even worse. He's confronting a whole class whose life-style of monied elegance — no matter how civilised, cultured and courteous — is a criticism of his own, a challenge to be matched in other ways. Win your five pounds a week extra for your men and that'll show you where all your fine culture'll get you and what you can do with it. It makes sense, I understand it, I can explain it and, as a trade union official myself, I even defend it. But, frankly, between thou and I, I loathe its spirit, its mean I'll-knock-you-down spirit.

ARTS PAGES

JOHN. ... It was Beethoven's violin concerto and Carl Orff's *Carmina Burana* and our music critic overheard one of the musicians saying, in a very loud voice: 'Now that we've buggered up Beethoven we'd better fuck Orff ... '

BUSINESS NEWS

MORTY. Tell me, Jane. That feature on dressing fat ladies, your model, where did you find her?

DOMINIC. Thinking of modelling fat men's wear are you?

JANE. The less we talk of that little fraud the better, I think.

MORTY. But she was beautiful. Fat, beautiful, happy and well dressed. Tremendous morale-booster for stout ladies.

JANE. But what those photographs didn't show, and we only discovered it afterwards, was that the clothes she was given to wear didn't meet at the back and had to be kept together with safety pins. She got hundreds of offers of marriage though.

NEWS ROOM

HARVEY. Right! My copy's gone down. *(To* LAYOUT*)* Sam, you laid out the new shape yet?

LAYOUT. It'll look like this. What's your headline?

HARVEY. Any ideas?

ANTHONY. How about 'Earnings I ain't got'?

HARVEY. He had earnings alright.

LAYOUT. How about 'Earnings: P.M. tells all'.

HARVEY. No. We'll keep it straight. 'P.M. I've still got an over-draft'. That's what he said. Will it go in?

LAYOUT. I think we can fit *that* in.

(MESSENGER *arrives with proof sheets.*)

HARVEY. Anthony, do me a favour and sub that for me, please.

SPORTS PAGES

MARVIN (*slamming down phone*). Another bloody adviser. Why do they always come through on a Saturday, the day when we're the only office working our balls off.

RONNIE. Occupational hazard, mate. Unlike the other depart-ments in this autocratic establishment we have democracy forced on us. *Everyone's* an expert on sport and every Sunday morning spiteful little eyes race down our columns in the 'let's-catch-'em-out game'.

NEWS ROOM

MORTY *arrives on the scene.*

HARVEY. Morty, your fink's story. Anything in it?

MORTY. The problem is, if a company like Onyx declares an overseas profit of £1 million they don't have to say where it comes from.

HARVEY. On the other hand don't you always do business with your friends?

MORTY. Right. That's what business is about, and Crafty Crafton was only going about his business.

E

HARVEY. Good. So we forget it.

MORTY. And a plague on all their houses.

HARVEY. Tony, that piece Chris did on Atlantis Insurance.

ANTHONY. All true, Harvey. Every word of it. But no documents.

HARVEY. We'll print it but it weakens the story without names.

ANTHONY. The old problem, loyalty to sources of information.

HARVEY. I bet there'll be a tribunal to investigate the collapse.

ANTHONY. Bound to be. And no doubt Chris'll have to appear and no doubt they'll ask him where he got his information from and he'll refuse to tell them and then, no doubt, they'll dismiss it all as hearsay. But what can we do?

HARVEY. My piece O.K.?

ANTHONY. O.K.

HARVEY. Good. We'll push out the first edition.

(Now the film on the backscreen becomes a film of the machines beginning to roll out the first edition. And with it comes the full blast of their noise which, though subsequently reduced for the remaining dialogue, continues till end of play.)

IN DEPTH

ANGELA *visiting.*

JULIAN. And so our ex-prime minister, Hotspur Hoskins as he was fondly known to us all, said of her, in one of his more jovial and confiding moods: 'Political commentator? Huh! That bitch'd get a scoop wrong if you gave it to her at dictation speed.'

ANGELA. Did he actually use the word 'scoop'? Jesus!

NEWS ROOM

HARRY *rushes in.*

HARRY *(calling* HARVEY *aside from main table).* Harvey?

HARVEY. What is it, Harry?

HARRY. I was right. There does exist a secret society.

HARVEY. Let's have it.

HARRY. It's hot.

HARVEY. Maybe, maybe.

HARRY. So prepare yourself for a burn because this one you won't want to print.

HARVEY. Well, let's have it, for God's sake.

HARRY. There's three people to a cell.

HARVEY. Yes, yes.

HARRY. And I'm sitting on top of an Angries cell when in burst three youngsters, nylon stockings over their faces, one carrying a gun, and they tell the Angries to lay off the violence.

HARVEY. With one of them carrying a gun?

HARRY. It turns out to be a water pistol.

HARVEY. Go on.

HARRY. So I trail the three rivals—

HARVEY. Make it short.

HARRY. And one of them turns out to be Mary's youngest son.

HARVEY. Oh no! Bloody hell! No.

ANTHONY. You're looking harassed, Harvey.

HARVEY *(to* HARRY*).* Tell him.

BUSINESS NEWS

JANE (*reading a letter*). 'And what's more,' she writes, 'I think you should not only be urging people not to have babies but you should encourage them to save our resources. Water for instance. I mean, soon the world will run out of water. Forgive the personal touch but *I've* stopped pulling the chain on my urination.'

DOMINIC. I see. Save our water and start a dysentery epidemic.

NEWS ROOM

ANTHONY. You can't tell her, Harvey.

HARVEY. Not in front of this lot, I can't. And it can't be *her* story either.

HARRY. You bet it can't. I've stood in the cold for days on this one.

ANTHONY. Don't be a fool, Harry. Yours is only half the ditty.

HARRY. Half?

ANTHONY. At this moment Saint Maria Mortimer is out gathering dirt which she believes will topple the dragon of Lannark.

HARRY. I don't connect.

ANTHONY. You should, my boy, you should. 'Only connect,' says Forster.

HARRY. I didn't go to university.

ANTHONY. I thought everyone went to university. She's in a pub, across the road, talking to an evil fink, who's offered her documents proving a link between Morgan King and your so-called secret society.

HARRY. Jesus!

ANTHONY. Well, Harvey?

HARVEY. I'm still thinking.

IN DEPTH

JULIAN. And so I walked into El Vino's for the first time in my life, 'cos everyone assured me I had to do my drinking there or I wouldn't know what was going on in the world, and I was thinking to myself: what a sad, grubby place this is, full of disappointed men and not a woman in sight to console them, and perhaps I'd come into the wrong profession after all, when a bloke comes up to me, pissed out of his mind, and says, as though he'd read my thoughts, he says: 'Pssst. A journalist is a man who possesses himself of a fantasy and lures the truth towards it – remember that and you'll go to the top.'

NEWS ROOM

HARVEY. Right! The bridges story comes back. (*Picks up phone.*) Frank? Don't hold that last edition. Yes, *don't* hold it I said. The bridges story stays in. Yes, in! In, in, IN!

ANTHONY. Harry, my boy, what you now do with your story is your own decision. Can you believe it?

FOREIGN DEPT.

MARTIN *rushes in.*
Urgent sound of 'tick-tack'.

MARTIN. There's something coming through on the telex. Jesus
Christ! Listen to this. 'The most horrific episode carried out
by the Mukti Bahani guerrillas of the newly formed state of
Bangladesh, took place today in the midst of celebratory
prayers which turned into cries of revenge for the 250
murdered Bangladesh intellectuals. The rally ended with
Islamic prayers in which five prisoners, whose crime was
alleged to have been an attempt to abduct two women from
a Dacca street, joined their captors in offering praise to Allah.
The crowd began to beat the trussed up men until a group of
the Mukti Bahani, wearing black uniforms, pushed them
back, fixed bayonets and began to charge the prisoners
themselves. They stabbed them through the neck, the chest,
the stomach. One of the guards, dismayed at having no
bayonet, shot one of the captors in the stomach with his
Sten gun. The crowd watched with interest and the photo-
graphers snapped away. A small boy of ten, the son of one of
the prisoners, cradled the head of his dying father, which act
infuriated the crowd who proceeded to trample on the child.'

NEWS ROOM

MARY *and* CHRIS *rush in.*

MARY. They're authentic. I knew it. Look.

CHRIS. True, Harvey. Front-page material.

HARVEY. It's too late.

MARY. Too late? You've held the last edition, haven't you?

HARVEY. It was too late, I tell you.

MARY. Too late? Too late? Whose nonsense is this? We agreed.

HARVEY. It came from the top. The bridges story had to stay.

MARY. Bloody hell! Didn't you tell them we had an important story coming up?

HARVEY. They wanted to see the evidence first. Too risky.

MARY. What cock and bull story is that, Harvey? *You're* the editor, aren't you?

HARVEY. And that's *my* decision.

MARY. But I promised I'd bring him down.

BUSINESS NEWS

JANE. Do you know, I never see any of you working. You're always standing around reading magazines with incomprehensible graphs and tables.

DOMINIC. Not work? My dear lady. First of all it's Saturday and our work's all done. Secondly I'm reading the opposition, and that's work. But that apart, do you realise the scope of our sphere of activity? Industry: subdivided into heavy, light, state-owned and private. Economic management. Industrial relations. International monetary control. The stock market, take-overs, interpretation of balance sheets, the impact of new technology. And *then*, all those headings are multiplicated, and hence complicated, when we deal with them on an international scale. Not *work*?

NEWS ROOM

MARY. I demand a better explanation, Harvey. That man's a politician and in the running to be on the party's executive. That makes him dangerous, a national risk.

BUSINESS NEWS

JANE. Surely you can't possibly attend to all those headings, there's not enough of you.

DOMINIC. Ah! *That's* a different question. What we *should* do is one thing, what we're *able* to do is another. I tell you, the cigarette packets carry a notice saying: 'Warning! Smoking can damage your health!' But what about all newspapers carrying a notice, on the front page, just below their names saying: 'Warning! The selective attention to data herein contained may warp your view of the world!' What about *that*, eh?

NEWS ROOM

MARY. But I could have brought him down. I promised you I'd bring that man DOWN!

ARTS PAGES

SEBASTIAN (*on phone*). No, no, dear fellow, you know it's much better to cut an entire paragraph rather than rearrange it. The printers invariably make a balls of it.

SPORTS PAGES

RONNIE (*on phone*). I can't help it. It'll have to wait over till next week. It's a small paper this week and fishing's a small sport – NO! I don't care if it does feed multitudes ...

NEWS ROOM

HARVEY (*to* SOMEONE). Get me some pulls of the News Digest, the bloody idiots have cut the wrong story.
MARY. He doesn't even listen to me now.

BUSINESS NEWS

JANE. I like it. 'Warp your view of the world.'
DOMINIC. Just below the name. Imagine it. 'The *Sunday Paper* – Warning! The selective attention to data herein contained may warp your view of the world.' Po-pom!

ARTS PAGES

SEBASTIAN (*still on phone*). Yes, yes. Your air tickets are in the post and they'll reach you in good time, now concentrate on the paragraph you're going to cut for me. How about the one comparing his playing to a 'flight of homeward-flying fleas'? Yes it may be accurate and funny but we do try to discourage our distinguished critics from being gratuitously offensive.

NEWS ROOM

SOMEONE (to HARVEY). The bridges story, Harvey, with the cartoon across four columns, it's too big.
HARVEY. What else is on the page?
SOMEONE. Look, here. Photo, diagram, cartoon, ad –
HARVEY. Cut the story.
MARY. Harvey, answer me!

IN DEPTH

JULIAN (on phone). Yes, the Atlantis story is going in, and it's a big story – very eye-catching – pretty diagrams and all that – most impressive. No! Of course no names are mentioned.

BUSINESS NEWS

JANE. *Daily Mirror* – warning –
DOMINIC. *The Times* – warning –
JANE. *Private Eye* – warning –
TOGETHER. 'May warp your view of the world!'

NEWS ROOM

MARY. HARVEY!

ANTHONY. Mary, my dear, look, I've got a problem ...

(*He takes her consolingly from the scene.*)

MARY. But why isn't he listening? He's not even listening.

Now, as they move off, everyone in all departments talks at once, a babble, a crescendo of voices melting into the full blast of the machines.

The sound continues but – the stage darkens – except for the bright image on the screen of the presses turning, turning, until they slowly dim to

BLACK

April 25th, 1972

A JOURNAL OF THE WRITING
OF 'THE JOURNALISTS'

The idea for the log-book came to me yesterday. The reason for keeping it is that it might produce material on which to base a series of lectures for delivery to university drama departments.

It might also, in the process, help to write the play by forcing me to clarify my intentions.

One aspect which I think will be omitted is the degree to which personal problems will cause blockages. However central to creativity peace of mind is, a distinction must yet be made between the problems inherent in the material and the external problems affecting a solution to them.

I think so, anyway. Perhaps it may not be possible. We'll see.

November 8, 1971

The idea for the play came to me after I became aware of the degree to which I found my own zest for work, public actions, and myself had become eroded by reviews, journalistic profiles, and columnists' attacks.

Having had the initial thought, I found other ideas creeping in: to what extent does the journalist damage himself when he engages in constant attack of others? Is there an element of self-destruction in him which is sufficiently true of other people to make him a subject for drama? Doesn't he reflect a special kind of mentality – which might be called lilliputian – which operates in all of us when we feel ourselves to be failures? He feels a need to 'cut down to size'. How often one encounters the mean-spirited person who feels compelled to reduce people to his own miserable stature. The journalist could be a mirror of that aspect of human behaviour.

Then, again, the setting of a newspaper is an opportunity to pursue many different stories and problems, to create many varied characters.

On March 4, 1971, nine months ago, I began making notes, a catalogue of ideas, character sketches, and passages of dialogue. On June 15 I started visiting the offices of the *Sunday Times* and made notes. These notes I dictated to my secretary over three days and produced fifty foolscap pages.

The idea occurred to me to write an article on journalism, which took me from August 31 to September 14. Two weeks. I typed it, sat on it, corrected, and added to it over a period of six weeks. The dictation of the notes and the assembling of them into an article were intended to help me familiarise myself with the material — at least. The article had an additional purpose of its own.

The first long period at the *Sunday Times* was broken by the summer holiday. After it — and after writing the main article — I went back to the offices in order to cover the Sport and Foreign departments. This necessitated changes to the article. I could have left out Sport and Foreign, but I felt nagged to be as complete in my researches as I could bear. (It became, towards the end, tiresome to keep going into the newspaper and hanging around, scavenger-like.)

The results of the sojourn at Thomson House were threefold. Firstly: I conceived the idea of giving the entire stage over to a structure which would contain the various sections, leaving just a centre space for action taking place outside the newspaper. It would be like *The Kitchen*, all sections going at once. This idea really excited me. I could begin to feel the shape of the play and had found a form which carried its own rhythms. Secondly: I accumulated dialogue, particular stories and atmosphere – I also, of course, learned of the technical problems and problems of industrial relationships.

But, thirdly, I picked up a doubt. My fears were confirmed that an essential part of the nature of journalistic activity was unknown to me. I had seen it operating at one level only – that of an outsider looking in, not as a practitioner. Would this matter? I didn't know how and still don't know. I'll only discover this as I go along.

In early 1970 I had wanted to write a major journalistic piece and I'd asked Harry Evans, editor of the *Sunday Times*, to lunch to tell him this, ask him whether it was possible, and to remember me if anything came up. What I'd really wanted to do was a series of profiles in depth of major politicians. A journalist friend had done this with German ministers for a German magazine: she'd spent three days with various ministers in their offices, homes, and restaurants to get an all-round picture. I'd tried to interest *The Times* but the Tory press office had told them I was politically unacceptable! Nothing came of all my efforts but in October 1970 I worked out a series of questions to present to ministers.

These questions now became the questions my journalist would ask ministers in the play – a kind of central activity while the rest of the drama was worked out. I tested the questions on one of the staff, who was very helpful.

With all this in the background I was now ready to start the play – at least I was equipped to, even though I personally may not have been ready. However, last Friday, I started.

Starting is always a problem, but glancing over those questions I found the opening: the journalist confronting a minister with a question about the nature of democracy.

I sat down to write the first complicated stage directions. To do so I needed to draw for myself a layout of the stage. With this drawing pinned on my desk in front of me I wrote the first page of dialogue. There I've stopped.

What is the first thing I find wrong?

November 11, 1971

First halted on page 2. Mary saying, 'Sir Roland, forgive me,' etc. Seemed too expositionary. But continued after a day to bottom of the page.

Now worried about the problem of dialogue that is both credible between a journalist and a minister and yet economical. In a way it's easy to be economical but it then becomes too pat. I think I must make him speak 'off the record'. His tone can alter and then there won't be a problem of 'is that the way and what a minister would say to a journalist?'

Also worried that this log will hold me up! With 17 pages written it seems to me that I've tackled the simple problems first — simply. I've alighted briefly on each section, touching each one to life, hinting in some places at the stories which grow and introducing most of the main characters.

The interviews with ministers.
The 'bridges' story.
The gynaecologist story.
The 'unseen' politician — Stormont Curtis-Brown,
    M.P. (what a name!), who will be the main target for Mary
    Mortimer.
The 'Angry Brigade' story.

What remains to be 'begun' is the 'strike story' and the 'science/politics' debate.

I've made up names as I've gone along, taking the first that has come to mind and only barely pausing to consider their sound. I'll check that later.

I've still got this fear that the dialogue has come out 'pat' but I reassure myself that I've been thinking about this play for nearly a year, have made notes over eight months and spent many weeks assembling actual dialogue exchanges in a newspaper office. Yet the fear is more substantial than that. It's almost as though the whole process of writing plays is no longer satisfying. There's no opportunity to be rich in expression, theatrical words seem thin. I enjoyed writing *The Friends* because characters had time to pause and express thoughts and feelings at length. I'd also established a form—no, a style of language, that could carry rhythm and sounds and, through those elements, atmosphere and feeling. Here, the very honeycomb structure permits only a superficial glance—or seems to. Perhaps it demands more incisive dialogue. So much needs to be established over such a large area in such a short time—two and a half, three hours?

The problem seems to be that I've chosen to play out the theme of 'self-destruction in a lilliputian personality' and I've set it in an arena which demands attention for many other stories and concerns. I'd love to make it work—but can I? Can *it*?

Anyway—though I keep wanting to pause and carve in character truths and clarify intellectual statements and shape out *some* degree of speech rhythm and pay attention to orchestration of mood and scene juxtapositioning—I keep pushing myself to *get it down* first, anyhow. There's so much to get down that even a bare structure is essential. After that I'll know a little more where I am and where the play is going.

The last scene I wrote this afternoon—of the three Angry Brigaders — worries me most. I've tried to glean the right atmosphere out of the prison letters of Ian Purdie and Jake Prescott printed in *Time Out* (August 20–26) and some of the

Angry Brigade notes. But already it has a different quality from
any of the other exchanges. I fear it's theatrical; on the other
hand I'm deliberately seeing them as melodramatic personages
who talk and cry mostly of love and brotherhood while plotting
to place a bomb in a school. I'm sure it's right to show such soft-
minded sentimentality at the heart of violence but the result is—
I don't know, odd.

November 17, 1971

In the evening, when I sat down again to write, I tackled three
problems: (1) Alterations to the Angry Brigade scene, to make it
say more, to divide up the dialogue, and give more of what
belonged to the different characters. (This is always a problem.
The voices in your head need sorting out. It's not always easy to
distinguish who is saying what, and so in the first drafts one gives
words belonging to one character to another.) (2) Introducing the
science and politics issue into the editorial conference. (3) How to
emerge out of the emotionalism of the Angry Brigade scene
back into the everyday havoc and banter of the newspaper.

In fact, this was the first problem. It was difficult to go on
from there. So I began to read through the notes in the leather
book and found the two 'computer stories'. Although they're
humorous, they're tender and slow. It seemed a good way of
easing back into the play. It was *then* that I knew the science-
versus-politics issue had to be introduced early on in the play as a
long-term issue which the newspaper was investigating. The
computer stories could appear on the women's pages—the 'light
end' of the paper.

(Lindsay Joe [Wesker's son] keeps telling me that the *Sunday
Observer* is a bad name for the paper: 'Can't have it, won't do at
all.' He's suggested the *Sunday Paper* instead. I quite like it. It's

straightforward, not a little trick to combine the *Sunday Times* and *Observer*.)

Begin today by deciding to divide play into acts and parts, rather than acts and scenes. Part One therefore becomes *Tuesday of Week One*, Part Two, *Wednesday of Week Two*, and so on. The problem with *that* time scale is that, though I think it gives me manoeuvrability, it is perhaps confusing. For instance: the bridges story handled by 'In depth' would normally be pursued over a week. I want the play to cover, at one and the same time, a week — in which the bridges story (and others) could make sense — *and* six weeks (for each day of the working week), by which time one would expect the bridges *plus* five other stories to have been handled.

How do I reconcile that?

Can I cheat and work on a time scale of *both* one *and* six weeks? Will that confuse? God knows. It's a licence I shall take, however.

November 18, 1971

Wrote most of Part Two yesterday, then realised Business News had been touched only once. In the process of working out an additional scene for them, just after half-way through Part One, I suddenly felt that I'd plodded my way along and that really I ought to establish a habit of quickly going from one section to another, perhaps just picking up only one sentence, and exclamation. It s a good device for speeding up passages, it also lends itself to humour and helps reflect the rhythm of the actual work.

All these passages of dialogue that I'd organised in the article were to hand for breaking up and distributing. So, I also added five little bits to Part One (I'm keeping a sheet of scenes written as I go along — so that also indicates afterthoughts).

The scene seemed to develop the science and politics debate

and to add to the growing battle between Mary and Curtis-
Brown, M.P. I also introduced the strike threat, developed the
bridges story, hinted at the Fink story.

So, we have these stories to control and bring together finally:

 (i) The interviews with ministers.
 (ii) The Curtis-Brown/Mary Mortimer conflict.
 (iii) The bridges story, which will switch to the gynaecolo-
       gist's story.
 (iv) The Angry Brigade.
 (v) The Biafra story.
 (vi) The politics–versus–science theme.
 (vii) The Fink story.
 (viii) The strike.

This leaves Women's Pages, Sport, Arts Pages without a main
story – although the strike will develop through the Sport
section, as the sports editor is father of the N.U.J. Chapel.

Also, I've yet to introduce Mary's children, who are grown
men and women belonging to another, more sophisticated and
less violent, militant group, and who must finally confront the
Angry Brigade.

It's perhaps too much – but I'll prune later.

Trouble is: last night I read over everything written and it
seemed unbelievably awful to me. Sketchy, with no direction, no
guts – just a bit of a game, an exercise.

November 19, 1971

Did very little yesterday. Wanted to get in a speech about 'fear
of making judgments', which became the Arts editor's contribution to the description of Mary. But in it were references to
'the intimidations by the artist', which Mr Curtis-Brown, M.P.,
is *not*. So, while wondering if the speech had relevance to the

play, apart from it giving another clue to Mary's character (but you don't need such a long speech to do that!), I suddenly thought of Andy in the *Golden City*, and the way they describe their city and I thought — let him echo Andy.

At the same time I thought that the conflict between Mary and Curtis-Brown (what a name! must change it) needed to be introduced earlier in the play. Bringing the two parts together gave me a new scene where the M.P. is reported making an attack on the layout of a 'new town' where he's been invited to open the new town hall.

And that's all I did.

But now the MS. is so full of alterations and additions, even at this early stage, that I'm contemplating doing something I've not done before, which is to type out what is so far written in order to give me a clearer picture of where I am.

November 22, 1971

Did very little on November 19 — half a scene, one where Mary dines with her three children, the once-a-month family gathering. But it seems a good scene: tight, funny, bringing her to life a bit.

Looking back over the notes I see that I first thought the initial introduction of the Mary/Curtis-Brown conflict should be over his 'order in chaos' quotation. Must try to fit that in. Also, this domestic scene is ripe for her 'I'm not "enbourgeoisé"' speech.

November 24, 1971

Had problems finishing the Mary/children scene. I wanted it to end up with her attacking them for persistently calling her bourgeois — using a 'definition-of-bourgeois' speech I'd written in the notes some weeks ago.

But it then seemed that she was right and her children wrong — which couldn't fit because they are to be the 'new guerrillas'. Not that characters can't be at odds, and be both sympathetic or unsympathetic, just that that unnecessarily confuses the already multifarious elements in the play. Until it struck me the next day that her self-defence unwittingly revealed *her* contradictions. When pressed and distressed she reveals a common ground with Curtis-Brown, the man *she* usually attacks, and it's *this* that her children point out to her. When she attacks him she attacks herself. She *is* engaged in self-destruction.

However, to help make this point I had to change the beginning of the scene and have them stumble across and read out from the proofs of her current column in which she's attacking another Curtis-Brown quote, which quote *she echoes* when pressed to defend herself against her children. It all made sense. I also reworked the structure of her speech, for rhythm and clarity.

Then on, all yesterday. Raced through seven pages, continuing the Fink story, computer stories, the abortion story, the strike, and character developments. But mostly it's colour — an organising, or, rather, a scattering around of some of the funny and vivid statements from the 'main article'.

All of which is very nice, amusing — great fun to select and scatter — but makes me feel that the dynamic is diffused. When you shoot off at amusing tangents, does it dissipate attention? At this moment I don't know. But I do know that the centre space scenes have too much in between them, and at this rate the play would stretch into six hours. So I have to give Mary another 'minister's interview' somewhere round about page 9 — half-way through Part One (as it's called at this moment). And I'll have to do the same half-way through page 2. It may help to tighten it up.

Now, the second minister must be very different from the first. At the moment I've not stated, specifically, whether they're from a Tory or Labour cabinet—though it should be possible to guess from the clues that it's a Tory one.

Another problem is that I want to cover so many subjects with them. Science and politics, art shaping the societies for which they must legislate, question of democracy, of their standards of living being so different from those for whom they legislate. Big questions and a large play—it makes me feel even more that I'm putting too much into it. Worry about that later.

Later: rotten work. Wrote the 'Angry Brigade' confrontation with the 'Long-Term Brigade' and I don't believe a word of it. I'm not really good at introducing thriller-type plots into my plays. Dostoevsky could have done it (did it); here it doesn't seem as though I've made it work. I can only hope that the sardonic tone comes off and that it's short enough to be lost in and sustained by the drive of the rest of the play.

November 26, 1971

Worked over that confrontation, made the Angries angrier and the Secret Brigade gentler, but that whole scene must be re-worked to contain more awkwardness, clumsiness.

Added three more ministerial interviews to break up the sections. And now I think I've come to the last section to take place mainly in the news room—the laying out of the paper during which the ends must be tied: the strike threat, the gynaecologist story, the revelation of Curtis-Brown as being behind the Secret Brigade—which Mary discovers—and her children being involved with Curtis-Brown, which Harry discovers. The discovery that Mary's children are involved becomes a problem for Harvey, the editor: should he go to press on it or not?

The Fink story must be dismissed, and actually the gynaecologist story should be handled *before* this last section so that it's a finished story, one way or the other, in the final layout.

Then I *must* type, because it's all too jumbled now for me to find my way about. I'll type it in a special way: give a page to each section so that it will make it easier to rearrange scenes, simply by switching pages.

November 29, 1971

It was a wise decision. At least I feel so at this moment. I did try to finish the play but it all seemed such a mess and I so disliked the confrontation between the two secret groups: it seemed so false that it paralysed me and I couldn't advance. The three new ministerial interviews came quickly because they were based on notes written in the previous months. (I have to keep reassuring myself that it's not unnatural to move so quickly and remind myself constantly that Handel wrote the *Messiah* in six weeks to pay for his mother's funeral – they say.)

As I type I make alterations and split up the longer sections in order to make the action move faster. The problem, as usual, is that there are so many ideas being thrown around that interest in them can only be sustained if they're not dwelt on. That seems a contradiction – after all, why shouldn't one dwell on an idea. But I suspect that audiences are prepared to listen to the exposition of a thought providing the structure of a play promises them variety. They'll listen, in other words, if they can see they're soon going to be taken on further.

I also find, as I'm typing, that new sections are required, either for rhythm, mood, or emotion. So that I'm constantly dipping into the *Journey into Journalism* article for passages of dialogue and adding them into the play. That article is like a pool of reserves. I can use it for anything.

Now, with each page containing a different section, I've got a pack of cards which can be shuffled around until the right rhythm, sequence, atmosphere is achieved. I can, as I go along, feel some of it by ear, as it were. But the main order can only be done when all the 'cards' have been 'struck'.

Now it's beginning to be exciting.

December 2, 1971

It's finished! The first draft anyway, yesterday. I feel I've not been as religious in keeping these notes as I'd hoped. Writing the play was more engrossing. But more than that I suspect there's remained in my subconscious an awareness of a degree of futility in the attempt. Had there been an intention to catch the thought process *as it occurred* – wires pushed in at the brain's point of output – that would have been valuable.

I look at a page of writing, page 44, with its crossings-out. Why the changes?

The word 'because' is moved to a different position because where it stood seemed to me literary, not vocal.

'You have' is changed to 'you've' – the same reason.

'Take off the masks' is made 'Take off those fucking masks'. The addition produces frustration as well as anger.

But a notebook such as this can't log each shift of thought. It's too tiresome. Yet each tiresome shift reveals the nerve-ends of the creative process.

The final intention became one of trying to bring together the important ends coincident with the beginning of the machines turning. It became evident that this must happen:

Mary must discover that her bête-noire, Curtis-Brown, was behind the secret society.

Another reporter must discover that her children were implicated.

She must push through her evidence unknowing of her children's involvement.

As it turns out, the editor does *not* hold the last edition to carry her story because he wants to save her from being the executioner of her children.

The question remains, should *he* be ignorant of the tie-up so that she *is* the executioner? That would be a starker enactment of her self-destruction but not true to the reality of the situation in which the editor *must* know what goes into his paper. The decision is his. And it would thus seem that she is *not* her children's executioner.

Put another way, if she was made aware of her children's involvement would she then have gone ahead?

But how relevant is it to put it this way? The facts remain the same. Curtis-Brown is still shown to be an idealistic side of herself with which she is uneasy and feels a constant need to attack. It occurred to me, though I'd not intended it, that it was right for her children to be part of this secret society because *they are also part of her.* And having realised this I added to Agnes's last words — where she points out to Mary how she, Mary, has just uttered a sentiment about the order of chaos which echoes something Curtis-Brown has said — the words: 'Mary, we're our mother's children. No escaping'.

It worried me a little that this was underwriting what was already implicit. But it sounded so much like myself saying it to my own mother. (Every time we quarrel about an individual stand I take I have to remind her that I'm her son; or when she calls me a fool for keeping such a costly open home I remind her again of how she did this in the East End — not costly, but always open, if only for tea — and that I've inherited it from her!) Also, if the line is delivered with the 'small laugh' as indicated, it becomes a touching attempt at reconciliation.

There is another problem which it's impossible to do much about: most of the Curtis-Brown quotes appear in the context of Mary's (or others') derision. Therefore they will emerge, in playing, as derisive. In fact, isolate them, write them down one after another on a separate page, and they merit serious consideration. It's like Ronnie in *Roots* appearing to most critics as a prig because they've not been thoughtful enough to lift what Ronnie says out from the tone of voice that is quoting him. This will happen with poor old Curtis-Brown: except that I've given him two champions - the Arts Pages editor and, of course, the children.

I'm still worried about the confrontation between the Angry Brigade and the Secret Society. It's clumsy and unreal. This morning I was reading excerpts in *Time Out* from the trial of Ian Purdie and Jake Prescott (who yesterday was sentenced to fifteen years for his association with the Angry Brigade: he'll appeal and get less, but it's a vicious sentence). While reading how the prosecution was trying to obtain Prescott's attitude to violence it struck me that he should have said: 'Why ask me about violence, the government you're defending is in possession of the arms of greater violence — not me'. So, as the Secret Society leave, Brian now yells at them such a question, pointing out that they are holding the gun. At which the first man tosses it to him telling him it was only a toy pistol.

Now this achieves some humour and takes the portentousness, or some of it, out of what they've been saying. It also adds dash and humanity to their personalities. But does such an action invalidate the question? After all, the military will not throw their nuclear bombs into our lap and declare them playthings, make-believe.

Still, I'm trying to do two things — get the question asked and give colour to the characters. I'm not sure if it works or if I'll need to separate the two. Actually, as I write, it strikes me that

I'll need to separate the two. Anyway, that scene requires the most work.

Then I needed to create a moment of calm before the storm, and added the scene where Norman and Cynthia talk about their inability to embarrass fools. It's a meditative moment but also adds to the description of Mary and gives them an opportunity to fill in their characters. Then, once the machines started, it seemed right for Tamara to have her outburst – as though the nervous breakdown she wanted was about to happen. Also *what* she talks about seems, obliquely, apposite.

One last major addition I felt a need to make was a straight lift out of *Journey into Journalism* – the last passage (my prose), which actually talks about the way in which toppling gods can lead to self-destruction. And it just seemed right to give this to the editor who, nagged by Mary to let her pursue the promised evidence against C.-B., feels it necessary to give her fatherly advice. The warning offered then becomes fulfilled. The piece gains inevitability.

This manner of talking about the play gives it a classical quality: mother devouring her children, destroying herself. But there lingers in my memory of the play (I haven't reread it yet – dare not!) a sense of slightness. I must get rid of this feeling that every sentence needs to have a weight and lyricism of its own. I almost can't bring myself to let a character say 'O.K.'. It's as though I've no patience with trivialities – I'll die soon, the world will end, I've not said what I mean, quick, hurry – and that's all wrong. Anyway, in this play I must force myself to accept that I've chosen an ultra-naturalistic setting and form. People *are* going to have to say 'Yes', and 'O.K.', and 'I beg your pardon'.

December 5, 1971

Should have left it alone for fourteen days not three! But I couldn't stay away. Made a chart for myself showing the positions of each scene. Discovered: that the Centre Spaces fell at fairly even intervals; that the play lasts perhaps two and three-quarter hours and not the four hours I'd feared, at least on a rough counting of the pages; that an interval could fall after the fifth Centre Space scene, leaving only two — fewer hold-ups, there-fore — in the second act. And then I read it! Christ! It just never took off. It seemed to flow, more so than I had thought it would, but I felt no — drama. On the other hand I could have been forgetting my own expectations from the setting. *The Kitchen* reads with difficulty, the impact of the movement and rhythm is only felt in production; perhaps it's the same with this play. Also, it's all *so* familiar to me now. I've lived in the offices of the *Sunday Times*, written up notes, and written the long article *all in this year*.

What I did discover and immediately rectify was that the Fink story was too widely scattered, so I've taken it all into the second act which tightens it up. I also cut out the second (Mr Cromwell) story and tightened up the last speech in the Angry Brigade/Secret Society confrontation and the editor's 'advice' speech.

Now I feel the ending is too hurried, too neat. It can't be dragged out any more, however.

I feel it needs to be read by someone who's quite fresh to the material, to see if they're gripped. But before I do that I'll go through with the aim of cutting and shaping some of the dialogue out of its prosiness. This evening I read simply to read it, to see what its overall shape was like. It was the first time. Up till now it had only been in my head and then thrown on to the paper. What I've just looked at is the first assembly.

Strange, but waking up, my memory of the play is not as bad as it was just after reading it. There's no logic in that, nothing's happened, unless it is that on reflection, although yesterday's reading didn't excite me as the incredible *tour de force* I'd imagined

I'd written, today's memory of it strikes me as *not* having been as bad as it could have been. No doubt a trick of the mind.

Now I must start by adding the little bits and pieces on this list. Next I must again read through *Journey into Journalism* to see if what I've left out is more important or relevant than what I put in.

I remember what I thought was wrong yesterday. The second act seemed to be just repeating the mood of the first: bits and pieces of stories flying back and forth between the different 'cubicles' — might be engrossing for a first act but can it be sustained for two acts? Only if the pace of the movement is increased (which will happen) *and* the pace, pulse, of what is happening and being *felt* between the characters is also increased.

So *what* pace is there?

1) The Fink story is introduced.
2) The freelance is getting more irritated about her gynaecologist story being ignored. Mary picks it up and moves it through — it follows her own confession about her and her father, which has depressed her.
3) The strike is threatening.
4) Tamara is becoming more and more frenetic.
5) The Secret Society grows.

Question: Can we introduce a film of mechanics preparing the printing presses — bolting metal plates, turning handles to release ink, etc.? It would create even more movement though the shots must be carefully selected, not *too* fussy or else they'll become too distracting — just calm printing men steadily setting up their very own beauties.

December 9, 1971

Tampered with bits and pieces but mainly left it alone these last days. Until last night, when I read the first act and really felt depressed. It was like a lumbering, dull animal unable to move and certainly unable to leap with that kind of energy an illuminating work of art should contain.

But I woke this morning determined to jettison something – to cut away what was holding the play down, rather like throwing weight out of the balloon in order to allow it to rise. In fact I've cut and reshuffled the pages between the first and second Centre Spaces. The decision to type out the different areas on separate pages *was* an inspired idea! It makes it so much easier to feel the rhythm – even visually, one can look to see how much type is on a page. If two fat pages follow one upon the other it's likely that the play lumbers at that point – not necessarily, but possibly.

So the first sixteen pages read more smoothly. It's a weighty scene to begin with, the interview with Sir Roland, launching the play straight into a heavy discussion of political concepts. But it doesn't last *so* long now, and it's followed immediately by short, sharp, funny scenes. Now I must continue to look for more cuts in the next section – between the second and third Centre Space. I'd actually like to get rid of one of the ministerial interviews. That might lighten the load.

Later: following on the second interview with Carron, Minister for Science and Technology, came an exchange between Gordon and Norman which continued the train of thought started by Carron. I cut that out completely. It had seemed right, as a kind of echo – from the minister back into the newspaper office – but again I felt we needed to return to the office in a lighter, more clipped, and episodic tone. So I reshuffled and placed four short funny flashes immediately after the interview.

Then I looked at the long editorial scene and realised that this too could be broken up into three sections, each divided by flashes from other departments.

F

This left me with the story about the Angry Brigade coming into the News Room as the ending to the second passage, leading into the Centre Space scene of the Angry Brigade itself.

So, the first two passages have been lightened. Now we go to the third passage prior to the end of the first act, which ends with Mary and her children.

Actually, on looking at the script, I realise that the third passage *doesn't* lead up to Mary and children and the *end* of the first act. Perhaps it *ought* to? There's an interview with the Home Secretary in between.

I could do this: combine the next two passages, so that it does lead to Mary and her children, and then *begin* the second act with the Home Secretary interview. This would make the second act begin as the first did. That might give the correct musical symmetry to the play. But I'm wondering whether the second act shouldn't at once start with an obviously faster rhythm than the first? We'll try it.

It also means cutting this third passage down—which I can immediately do by cutting out the Stevenson [a character Wesker subsequently dropped] story. It's allegorical, a sort of commentary on the science and politics debate, but it's also part of the ballast holding the play down. I don't think we need it. Four Centre Spaces and three passages is enough for a first act. I like that shape.

Later: the big problem was what to follow the emotional Angry Brigade scene with. It couldn't be anything funny—that would have seemed to be laughing cheaply at what should be treated seriously in order to attack it effectively.

So I thought of the scene in the Foreign department with the noise of the telex machine jumping through a Curtis-Brown quote. The sound is a sharp, urgent one—a good leap from the intense sentimentality of the Angries' violence. But the quote itself dealt with a government communicating with its people. It seemed a wrong issue to follow on, too strident. Something mellower was needed.

So I thought of exchanging it with an earlier Curtis-Brown quote about building a compassionate society for imperfect men. It was shorter, more personal, and seemed to cast back pity upon the anguished young anarchists.

Then I simply laid out the remaining thirteen sheets over the desk and along the couch and looked down at them, trying to draw from them a sense of their correct order.

In this passage it was obvious that the humorous story of the bridges could be the back-bone. I decided to make every other flash an In depth/bridges flash, interspersed with mood flashes into sport (the naming of sons after pubs) and Foreign (Gordon talking about growing old), then increasing the tension of the passage by building in the strike story and introducing the secret society story towards the end. But I couldn't end on that, otherwise it would take away from the Mary/children scene which was the real climax. So I brought down the temperature by having Jane and Angela talk about ideas for series, with its contemplative final observation about newspapers only being places filled with people waiting for ideas to come to them.

But this left the major problem of the large flash into the Arts Pages where Sebastian has his long monologue on Mary. Can this third passage – after two interviews and an Angry Brigade scene – sustain such a long monologue? Especially when there's still one more Centre Space scene to go and a long one at that? We'll see. Perhaps we won't know till we're in rehearsal.

Anyway, it's exhilarating working this way. It's extraordinary how rewarding it is to jettison passages. Though I've always known this. It's creative in the way editing a film is creative. And laying out pages on a surface is actually very like hanging up lengths of film; I'm looking at 'separate frames' and juxtaposing one with another.

December 22, 1971

Thirteen days elapse. I hadn't intended to leave it alone for so long, but John Dexter came to discuss *The Old Ones* and threw out a suggestion for a change which at first I thought was a good idea but which, on sitting down to write it, ended in paralysing me. I both couldn't make it work and lost the drive I'd worked up for *The Journalist*. So I decided to put away *The Old Ones* and return to this one to try and get a copy ready for the Aldwych to have a look at. I'd promised them a draft by the end of this month.

So, I've just read it through. The first time in its new order. I'm relieved. The rhythms now work and the stories develop more evenly. That is to say, it all seems to flow and fit into the structure I've conceived; but what I'm not certain about is whether or not the whole conception is *ill*-conceived. I've cut out the last line, 'Have pity on yourself, Mary', which sounded melodramatic, but I have a suspicion it might all be *too* carefully constructed.

On the other hand, it occurs to me that the less possible it is to reconstruct your set on stage (how can you really encompass a newspaper building on a stage?) the *more* you're pushed into stylisation, which in turn demands a greater degree of contrivance. The question is: how easily can the delicate theme of self-destruction sit in the stern framework of a densely populated, highly stylised stage set? I need someone else to tell me that.

Now I want to introduce one last strand into the web of stories: the story of this terrible Pakistan war. Beginning with the military massacres in East Pakistan, the flight of six million refugees into India, the swift Indo-Pakistan conflict leading to the establishment of Bangladesh, and the discovery of the last minute slaughter of the 280 Pakistan intellectuals, and ending with the revengeful public torture and murder of four suspected collaborators in that massacre. The son of one of these four was seen to be cradling his dying father and the crowd trampled on him also. The priests have a lot to answer for!

December 29, 1971

Finished typing second typed draft last night, six days. Then meticulously 'holed' sheets — three copies, 345 pages — and clamped them into folders. This morning I will read it. As usual, I fiddle with telephone calls, making coffee, and perfunctory clearances before facing the read-through.

Will the slipped-in passages relating to the Indo-Pakistan war work? Is it now too heavy, too full? Are there now too many lumps of dialogue which are simply quotes from newspapers? Has the balance been shifted? I come across a note in my notebook referring to the unions and strikes which I've now typed, and am waiting to see where it can be slipped in. While typing I made changes — broke up passages, rendered 'prose' into a 'spoken' language, and clarified.

The confrontation with the two secret societies works better now — though whether that's due to changes or simply that I've gotten used to it I don't know. I think I'm happier because I've sorted out the voices more distinctly. The First Man now talks with impatience and obviously despises the Angry Brigade. Jeremy is obviously the impetuous fanatic. The characters seem individual. There's also argument of some merit from the A.B. and I've cut down that 'last speech' to a few lines.

February 3, 1972

Five weeks later. David Jones came to discuss the play today. We spent four hours together. As it was only a second draft I'd shown him, I felt the need to talk first and say what direction I thought the third draft would take.

1) The normal process of tightening up dialogue for rhythm and truth-to-character reasons.
2) Development or filling out of some of the characters, such as the various editors.
3) The ending. I wasn't sure if it was too melodramatic or whether another 'moment' was needed in order to show that the machine went on and on.
4) The major worry: the 'truth' of the Angry Brigade-secret society scenes.

It was this last which was the major worry for him. Was it in fact a distraction, another play? He felt that the confrontation with the ministers worked perfectly, but that on the other occasions when one wandered away from the office then he was irritated, it was a hold-up.

Trevor Nunn and Terry Hands had, with reservations, liked it and felt they should go ahead and contract it and trust me to produce a workable third draft. Ronald Bryden, ex-*Observer* critic and now their 'dramaturg', thought it was my best since *Chips* but had minor reservations, as a journalist, on some of the dialogue which he said, if I wanted, he'd go through and offer advice upon. Also, he said that one of the major preoccupations among journalists was the issue 'fact equals truth', and this seemed missing. I told David that this was curious since it was a major concern in *Journey into Journalism* and I was surprised that I'd bypassed it in the play.

Other points he made were:

1) He wanted to see more of Mary, the central character.
2) He wanted to hear dialogue that was rather in relation to specific assignments than 'sitting back' comments.
3) Could there be greater use of real names in addition to Weinstock?

4) He wanted to see more happening in 'sports'.
5) He was worried that *all* Mary's children were in the secret
   society — rather like the three musketeers.

With these, in addition to the reservations I had led off with, I
think I agree.

The problem was what could happen to the Angry Brigade
scenes. I was not certain whether I'd simply not made them work
or whether they just couldn't ever be made to work because they
were trying to cover an inherently too vast field of conflict. We
agreed that I ought to face the possibility that they'd need to
come out entirely. And as we talked a vague alternative emerged:
the last comment David had made was that he would like to have
seen an issue brought up in an office, followed through 'outside',
and then have watched how the truth of the reality of that issue
was forced to change because of the demand of journalism.

I liked this idea, especially as it tied up with one of my early
notes which I'd ignored — and also I could perhaps salvage some
of the Angry Brigade issue (about which I felt strongly) and use
it in a different form. In the process it might throw up the other
forgotten preoccupation of the journalists about the different
natures of truth and fact.

In all it was a good, helpful, and reassuring meeting. I asked
David to consider signing a contract now, which I think he'll
persuade the R.S.C. to do.

February 16, 1972

Talked with John Dexter some days ago about the play. He liked
it in a general way, but (while saying he had only read it once
and usually only feels confident to pass judgment after two or
three readings) made two major observations. One, he couldn't
see the point of going outside the office at all to the Centre Space

scenes. But maybe this was due to his second observation: to do with focus. By focus I think he meant that the play doesn't begin with the right first scene. He said it may simply be a question of reshuffling scenes, or that it would right itself when the character of Mary was filled out.

The question of focus is, however, important, and I'm now toying with such ideas as beginning with the 'family' scene. Anyway, I've delayed working on the rewrites to do something I've never done before – that is, write a new play! In the last eight days I've got down the first draft of *The Wedding Feast* – the play I'd wanted to make out of the Dostoevsky story which I'd written as a film script five years ago.

It fell neatly into place because most of the work had already been done in the film script. With that out of the way, I plan to approach the rewrites as follows. First of all, to reread *Journey into Journalism* and make notes on usable dialogue or incidents which I'd forgotten about. Then to work on the filling out of minor characters. Next to introduce additional incidents. Finally to look at the question of focus and the character of Mary.

February 17, 1972

Absolute dry-up. I read the 'Journey', made notes, and then could do nothing. Momentum lost. Total lack of interest in the play. Not one character seems either important or interesting, and certainly I could feel no enthusiasm for putting a newspaper on the stage. So I spent the evening wandering around the house and watching the inanities of *Task Force* on TV. Not even the sports programme moved me. My brain felt vegetable and leaden. Apart from a few thoughts straying to the play I couldn't even bring myself to think about it.

Could the family scene open the play? It ends with an emotional outburst – can't have that so early in the play. Should we begin with the editor? Centre more things around him? Is that the correct focus? It all seems too big a task. Perhaps I've just worked too much, too fast, and need recharging on something? What?

Later: perhaps the question of focus is more to do with content than with 'who'. It could be both, of course. I started off by wanting the play to explore the theme of self-destruction. In the process, faced with the opportunity offered by a newspaper setting, I hoped to include and enrich the canvas by touching on many issues and creating innumerable vivid characters. Let it throb with ideas, people, and action.

But now what has emerged is a main thread which explores the nature and problems of democracy. The interviews with the ministers do this, the statements of Curtis-Brown touch on it, the references to the Pakistan war highlight it in an extreme way, and the very nature of journalistic activity involves considerations of social responsibility and the extent to which one should frustrate or encourage public action. Perhaps this is what needs tightening up.

March 1, 1972

Three weeks later: should have kept a daily diary. But roughly: spent a week in Wales with family and gave it a rest. Though on the last day began to write.

The method of writing each department on a separate page proves more and more valuable. For example, I decided to give body to the character of Norman by making him slightly hypochondriac, and suggesting he was one of those journalists who constantly want to get sent abroad in order to escape a messed-up marriage. It was much easier to write, on separate pages, the passages of dialogue that would build up such a character and then intersperse these throughout the manuscript at the relevant places. I could pursue the development without worrying about the scenes between.

In these last three days I've jettisoned the two scenes involving the Angry Brigade and the Secret Society. Instead I've made Harry talk about their existence so that it's become an 'assignment' to pursue. Also, I'm playing with another idea in which it's discovered how Curtis-Brown is tied up with them. The editor announces he's having a lunch with Curtis-Brown and Mary is eager to know what his impressions are. In reporting back he quotes some odd words used by Curtis-Brown (pinched from *Golden City*), and these words turn up again in a note from the Secret Society to strikers to whom they're giving funds. Betrayed by a verbal slip. It might work.

Also, on the question of focus, I've brought Mary into the newspaper office sooner, so that her 'profiles' are made to appear central to the overall discussion the editor wants to pursue: science versus politics. I've also built in more scenes involving her so that the focus is now, without doubt, on her – the journalist. In addition, by taking away the Angry and Secret Society scenes from the Centre Space, the Centre Space scenes which remain all involve Mary: the interviews and the one family scene.

Other characters have been built up. Cynthia – aware, intelligent, with a feminine concern for a photographer whom she thinks they're brutalising by giving him only scenes of violence to photograph. Paul, who I've made an older man representing the old, more conservative, guard. And other dashes of personality here and there. With so many characters it's a real problem to make everyone full-blooded. The nature of the play permits mostly impressionism.

I've also increased the range of subject matter, perhaps too richly; but the aim was to ensure that the serious pursuits and achievements of journalism were represented alongside its destructive, flip side.

And the editor. I've planted him firmly as the first character to speak in the newspaper office, which both strengthens his character and contributes to the focus. He's the head, people come to him with ideas, ideas flow out from him.

I'm now seriously worried that either there's too much (but I'll look at that later) or that there will *appear* to be too much because I've cut down the breakaways to the Centre Space from seven to five. Though I don't think that. Seven breaks from the office rhythm was probably too irritating. Five should work.

The rhythm, now that so many new scenes are introduced and other shifted around, is completely shot to hell. Length and rhythm are the next major concerns. Again, I shall have to lay all the pages out on the floor and look at them that way.

March 2, 1972

Today, on the back of a huge *Friends* poster, I drew out a chart of 120 squares and wrote in the present order of scenes.

First of all I realised that there were few Women's Pages scenes throughout and only one in part two. I'll still have to attend to that, if it's necessary. Then at the end of the play, when the Sports are having the busiest time of any section, there were no sports scenes. So I wrote some in and transferred one.

My next problem was placing the scenes in which Harry gives Mary her clue about Curtis-Brown and she then communicates it to Harvey. This necessitated pushing back the News Room scene between Paul and Harry to before the interval. Which was better anyway, as I need a long time-lapse for Harry's return.

But the most important reshuffling was needed when I decided to change the last line—or rather I saw another way of ending the play which eased my concern about the melodramatic ending. I broke up the last News Room scene, interspersing it with Sports scenes, and also broke up Mary's cry of 'I could have brought him down'. She says it once; then I reshuffled Norman's odd passage about being embarrassed by fools; then Mary demands an explanation; then comes the Cynthia passage about the 'boy born for abuse' – as though lengthening the last chord; then back to Mary with her final 'I could have brought him down' – and then, to throw her complaint into relief, the quote about the last massacre. And for the last line I brought forward the line which ended the first part – Cynthia asking Norman doesn't he feel guilty for confusing without offering real help. 'Constantly.'

Now. Is *that* too neat? I feel that if the noise of the press machines is brought up and people move and talk more energetically then it will have the ragged feeling, the sense of continuing, which I want.

Anyway, I must leave the new order alone and read it tomorrow; or I'll have something to eat now and dally around the TV and then read tonight.

March 5, 1972

A friend came to stay for the weekend: at 42 she's to take a late degree in history, and we mulled over an essay on the Chartists that she was having difficulty with. It set me thinking more about revolutionary movements and the rhythms of their rising and falling and it struck me that possibly the kind of mind and energy needed to agitate, violently or otherwise, is different from that needed to reconstruct; and once the fighting is over and it's clear who's won then a new breed steps in – often the honey-mouthed opportunists. Last night, I met with some writers who surround the *Jewish Quarterly*, and someone spoke about the phenomenon of hatred that exists for artists and intellectuals – rather as Tamara speaks of the awful pointer there was in the Pakistan murder of the intellectuals. And again I was reminded that this is the central preoccupation of the play, and that the editor must make such a point to Mary – one that would give cohesion to the entire play. So I added a piece to the confrontation, at the end, between him and Mary. And this is what I really believe the play to be about.

And it *is* complex, this time, now, its frighteningly complex. New states being born, new classes and races finding their voice, feeling their strengths. A time ripe for opportunists who can mouth the platitudes of pain and suffering and passionately conjure up the horrid sweetness of revenge. And anything can happen. It can swing one of two ways – a glorious release of all that's noble in men or a murderous unleashing of savage spites and envies. And we have the power to tip it one way or the other; not simply by what we say, but the way we say it. The habit of knocking down giants is very seductive and contagious, we're very good at being spiteful. I'm not all that proud of the history of journalism, Mary, and I don't want to see the *Sunday Paper* perpetuating it.

This led me to feel that the ending is still not the right one. For Cynthia to observe how newspapers inundate us with information, thus encouraging a sense of impotence, is not strong enough – especially with Norman's reply of 'Constantly' as the last word. Much stronger would be Dominique's sardonic suggestion: 'Warning, the choice of information herein contained can be a danger to your view of the world.'

And in the morning's *Sunday Times* is a eulogy of Hughie Green in which, with depressing and distressing familiarity, he talks of the 'people counting', sounding just like a politician and thus perpetuating – elevating – ordinariness. I'm going to use that. So that means we'll have the theme of democracy, or 'the manipulation of people', or whatever, tackled from government (the ministerial interviews), industry (the references to Arnold Weinstock), and popular entertainment (this reference to Hughie Green).

March 11, 1972
Letter to David Jones:

Here is the third draft. It's long. It's very long. But, I feel it must be. The canvas is so large. The canvas of a newspaper is so large. Think of all the different issues one's forced to consider on a Sunday. I know they have all day — but then we haven't tried to cover a whole newspaper! I think this should be set up as a long play, talked about as a long play, anticipated by the audience as a long play. Providing the image on each frame (there's about 150 to flick your eyes around at), providing the content of each frame is compelling enough, then why shouldn't an audience be riveted for three hours? It's a meaty play, let them come away exhausted but at least for a substantial reason. A huge bite. A two-hour play, if it's mediocre, can also seem endless. It's going to require a lot of rehearsal to get spot-on timing and the right rhythm. I just feel we should approach it as an exciting marathon.

However, you'll see that I've eliminated the two 'Angries' scenes. Most, if not all, characters are fuller. I've even given a few minutes to secretaries. All the Centre Scenes are therefore given entirely to Mary, no other diversions. And I've built the editor into a more central figure so that he becomes a more focal point to the paper's activities. In fact, with his build-up and Mary's build-up there is greater focus to the whole play.

You'll also notice that I've changed that melodramatic ending and tried to create a kind of elongated musical ending. I'm not sure that it works; on reading, it may seem like fits and starts. But each of the last 'frames' has an oblique reference to the cry 'I could have brought him down'.

It may be that some cutting could take place, and it's for sure that some reshuffling of the 'frames' will be needed. I'm by now too close to it. But some of that can take place on paper, the rest I suspect will have to take place in rehearsal.

I hope you like it. It's certainly richer. Bryden can put his mark on this draft if he likes and I'll be grateful for his advice.

April 20, 1972

Six weeks later: Ronald Bryden, now 'literary editor' to the R.S.C. came yesterday to talk about his suggestions. They fell mainly into two parts: authenticity of dialogue and structure. We were together from 11 a.m. till 4 p.m. He was very helpful.

The confrontation had its curious side and I had to remark on it. We can't pretend that I didn't go into a detailed criticism of your review of *The Friends*, I told him ['Casual Condemnations', in *TQ2*, 1971]. He said he'd planned to write a friendly reply and told me how working as critic for the *New Statesman* gave him just that extra time to get a better perspective on a play.

He was in a strained situation and handled it with a nice mixture of grace, nervous modesty, and cunning. After all, he was not simply the critic who'd disliked *The Four Seasons* and *The Friends* but, as he confessed towards the end, felt defensive as a journalist. From which came his most important observation, which is true and which I want to find place for in the play: that journalists don't simply knock down giants, they often create them and then knock them down to make room for others – so they *do* celebrate but what they celebrate is novelty, fashion.

This of course doesn't deny that giants (it's becoming an irritating word) do emerge in their own right, without help and because of their natural artistic, intellectual, or other powers – and *they* attract hostility. Also, of course, the play is presenting a human state of mind, not merely a journalist's. Nevertheless it's a valuable comment in view of the play's choice to work out its theme through the setting of a newspaper office.

But the most surprising suggestion was the one for changing the title (David is apparently also going to suggest it when he comes to give his 'notes' tonight). 'Something about *The Rise of The Meritocrats*'. He'd read a book once, in 1950, by Michael Young, with a similar title, which he thought very prophetic, and that the play was proving the prophecy. The question posed by the book, he said, was what shape would the country take when all the post-war youngsters, who'd been given greater educational opportunities, reached positions of power? Many would be from working-class or middle-class backgrounds who'd make it on their merit rather than through the influence of their backgrounds. And here they were, in this play, Oxbridge men and women who'd reached influential positions in journalism.

That he saw this as being what the play was about threw me somewhat. I just hadn't seen the characters in these terms, nor was I concerned to chart a particular phase in educational history. Such an observation could be syphoned off from the play's many waterways but could the source I'd gouged out be *so* lost? Am I mistaken about the theme of the lilliputian being echoed throughout the play's caverns?

Spoke with my sister about it last night. She brought up two main points. The first coincided with Vera's [Vera Elyashiv, to whom the play is dedicated] – wanting to know more about Mary. The other repeated another of Bryden's suggestions: that Mary should actually be seen hearing the news of her son's involvement in the Secret Society. I think I must add one or two more details about Mary's life, but to have her face the knowledge of her son's relationship with the Society would a) throw up more problems than there is time to solve, b) be too melodramatic, and c) detract from the intention of ending with the image of the newspaper going on and on, regardless of criticism and misfortune. But more: there is another dimension achieved, which I can't name, when you have her raging for Curtis-Brown's downfall while unknown to her is unfolding a grim picture of her son's future.

One last detail brought up by Bryden threw into focus an aspect of playwriting which momentarily embarrassed me: Carron's speech touching on 'La Belle Époque' refers to the theories of Adam Smith and Darwin gaining recognition in that time. The reference is one I picked up from a source that I've since forgotten but Bryden was arrested by the two names since there's a hundred years between them. It didn't worry me at the time because I assumed that La Belle Époque was a period in which many things came to be accepted, including a back-log of theories. But his probing reminded me how one makes characters refer authoritatively to events and ideas about which one is not oneself an authority. I shall chase back on that issue (futurology I've read quite a lot about), but the question arises whether one needs to be as erudite as the characters one is creating. I have a layman's sketched-in picture of history but need I be an authority? If the play were *about* La Belle Époque, yes, naturally I'd need to research. But for a passing observation? It was red-face-making, however.

April 21, 1972

David came last night. His comments were few. Basically the second act worried him. He accepted my point about retaining the irony of Mary not knowing of her son's impending crisis, but made the valid observation that between pages 105 and 130 (25 pages) there was no reference to the spinal story of Mary versus Curtis-Brown. He felt that during those pages the 'story' aspect of the play, its cementing quality, had slipped into diffusion. I think he may be right.

Next: that when Harry comes to the editor with the news

about Mary's son, everything from then on happens too quickly. We need a break between the news and the decision what to do next. Again, I agree.

Lastly, aside from two or three minor comments: the way I've counterpointed the ending. I was well aware of the risk I'd taken and he too was uncertain it would work. He felt that a) The passages *in between* Mary's expostulations were too long, and wouldn't achieve the effect I wanted of the newspaper rushing inexorably on – the length holds up the flow; and b) following on from that, those passages were more concerned to tie up thematic loose ends rather than to illustrate a paper at work in its final stages. My reply was that, in reading, one was forgetting the bustle and rush going on elsewhere, emphasised by the film and noise of the presses themselves. He said 'maybe'. I said I'd look at it and perhaps write out two alternative endings.

My suggestion to call the play *The Journalists* – in the plural – was accepted; it was a better title and detracted from the idea that the play was only about Mary.

April 25, 1972
Letter to David Jones and Ronald Bryden:

I've worked on nearly all your combined suggestions – I think they helped the play, though I confess to being worried that I've lost a daring – albeit risky – ending (rhythmically speaking). I've left all the corrections in by hand, so that you can skim through the play and glance at the handwriting in order to see what I've done. Except for Sebastian's big speech which, David will be pleased to see, is cut; that one is typed. The following are the major rewrites:

1. The title is changed to the plural.

2. Curtis-Brown is changed to Merlin King, M.P.

3. Ron's plea to strengthen the theme of 'the rise of meritocracy', although it's not an issue that I find more than passingly interesting,

*did in fact sink into me and as I read the play I could see all the clues
in it which lead him to focus on it. I hope what I've done pleases him
and gives the play strength. Anything that's true must help and I do
recognise the validity of his observations.*

*4. Also his much more, for me, perceptive point about journalists
building up giants. I've used that to infiltrate more humour!*

*5. 'La Belle Époque ... Adam Smith ... Darwin'. I suddenly re-
membered my source. I'd spent weeks reading that huge tome* The
Year 2000 *by Kahn and Wiener, and the passage comes straight from
them. Yes, Adam Smith and Darwin in the same breath. However,
if it made Ron gasp then it's best left out and you'll see that in
rewriting the passage I've made it an even clearer statement.*

6. Ron's suggestion that the strike be brought in earlier — done.

*7. But his suggestion that the Pakistan war be prepared for — well, it
had been! On re-reading I discovered that part three ends with
Gordon reading out excerpts from the Pakistani leader's war speech:
'"My dear countrymen, peace be with you," he said in his speech
announcing war ...'*

*8. David's point about the news of Mary's son and the reaction to it
happening too quickly — that's broken up and leads to a solution of
his other point —*

*9. About the ending needing to happen more under pressure of work
than pressure to 'thematically tie up the ends'. I'm curious to see how
you both respond to the new ending.*

*10. David's very important observation about the enormous gap
between the last reference to the Merlin King story and its reintro-
duction towards the end I've solved by simply shuffling them closer
to each other rather than writing in new scenes. I'm becoming a
leeetle worried about the length.*

May 1, 1972

Rewrites are all fine. David gave me final suggestions last night

All helpful. Merlin King changed to Morgan King – for obvious reasons!

May 4, 1972

Yesterday morning, on the front page of *The Times*, was the announcement that women had been allowed into the Stock Exchange. This meant that the very first story in the play was already out of date, even before being roneoed! I changed it at once and telephoned the revision through to Odanti. But the incident launched a fit of depression which grew in proportion to my diminishing estimation of the play's value. I'm filled with such an unbearable sense of its ordinariness.

I've also been reflecting on the various changes with which I imagined I agreed. Both Vera and David felt something was wrong with the first interview. Vera was specific and said the journalist would show some modesty, would flatter the minister, draw him out. So, I gave her a degree of 'feigned' modesty and in the rewriting clarified the threads of the argument. Now I feel a certain crispness is lost. Before, the statements were bold, huge chunks, classically hewn and juxtaposed, with no intention to add the stammerings and shynesses of natural conversation. They didn't seem necessary, I wanted to place down only the primary colours of the debate. There now seems such a prosaic quality to it.

Similarly: Bryden's suggestion that Anthony wouldn't say, 'Always seems to me that health authorities are very much on the ball', when referring to Harvey's blowing up of the cholera epidemic – 'don't believe in epidemic scares'. Bryden says it sounded too 'benevolent'. A likelier journalistic objection would be: 'The agencies always launch them with mortality figures in the hundreds and three days later they've whittled them down to ten or twenty'.

The Bryden suggestion is possibly nearer to a 'journalistic objection to epidemic scares' as he puts it; but my piece of dialogue catches a glimpse of the person. Bryden makes him accurate, I make him sensible. Bryden makes him testy, impatient, I make him reliable, paternal, an anchor—he seems to have an understanding of people. After all, why should a health authority give itself headaches by letting some cholera cases grow out of hand? Bryden's suggested line reveals less interesting personality traits: a comment on agencies, a desire to be (not all that) funny. And, odd, because had I written it I can see him putting up the objection: would Anthony make a comment about agency behaviour to an editorial conference of colleagues who'd know all about agencies? The difference is subtle but perceptible—my line came with unthinking instinct; my agreement came only after being 'thoughtful'! That's not to claim instinct above thought—but caution, caution.

JOURNEY INTO JOURNALISM
A very personal account
in four parts

Contents

Preface — 1972

There was a moment when I seriously considered not publishing this small book because the material for it was gathered for another reason: as a background setting for my play *The Journalists*. It seemed I was cheating.

I had asked, and was generously granted, permission to wander freely through the offices of the *Sunday Times*. But I couldn't resist shaping the notes made there into a piece of journalism. Surely, even if no one published it, the organisation of scrawl into a coherent shape would assist in the writing of the play. It did. Fortunately, my publisher also liked it.

Although most of the quotations come from journalists working on the *Sunday Times*, some do not. It would be too pedantic to distinguish who said what, nor does it matter. I wanted to evoke a newspaper atmosphere as well as describe particular events – and so I've chosen this mixed form, of sequence and montage; sometimes the record is chronological, sometimes one passage draws together many statements uttered at different times by different people.

I'm very indebted to Harry Evans, the editor. He didn't think it incumbent upon me to ask for permission to publish it but it was important to me to receive his blessing before agreeing to let my publisher go ahead. He gave it despite having, naturally, very strong criticisms. Considering that I became simply another headache added to all those confronting an editor, he has been courteous (if firm about certain aspects of the piece), helpful and finally very just.

London
July 1972

Preface — 1977

Since writing that first preface, almost five years ago, a great deal has happened. So much that inevitably one asks: is it too late for the book to be published? I don't know but wish to take the risk. A book on journalism is/was the largest writ invitation to criticism, but because publication was held up there is the added risk of anti-climax: what was all the fuss about?

An explanation of the delay is necessary. On pages 204 to 217 I've written the story within the story, of how I got certain things wrong and was sternly corrected. I've not only recorded the telling off but have shown how I went wrong and added the corrections in the critics' own words — my mistakes and the manner in which they were corrected were, after all, also part of my 'journey into journalism'.

These additions failed to satisfy, or pacify, at least, two of the journalists on the staff. I made a vow to myself that, because I'd gained entry into the building in order to collect material for a play, I'd publish only if everyone with whom I'd spoken agreed I could publish the slim volume. It was a self-imposed restriction. For five years the objections remained. Then in a TV interview with Melvyn Bragg, when asked in connection with freedom of the press 'What about the Wesker book?', Harry Evans implied there were no longer any reasons why it shouldn't be published. He turned to the camera and said, 'You can go ahead and publish, Arnold!'

I do so, and offer the work with the words of the late Nick Tomalin: 'You got it as right as any of us ever get anything right!'

London
January 1977

PART ONE

> 'There's no role for this country to perform, so
> where do the best minds go? Not politics or the
> civil service — journalism instead. They can't legislate
> or exercise power so — they comment! Journalism
> as an act of creating self-awareness in society.'

The beginning

I have been told: 'You can come any time, sit in, see anything.'
The purpose: I'm contemplating writing a play with a newspaper
background. *The Times* Diary hears of the story and a reporter
phones me to ask the odd gossipy question, I tell him I want to
avoid creating a cliché setting. Some days later they write up the
story and invent a quote: 'He (Wesker) calls his stint "living in
the atmosphere of printers' ink" — that's a cliché he might
avoid … ' I wince at the lie but am reminded why I want to
write the play.

The reception area is designed by Lord Snowdon out of blocks
and lines of type-face in different sizes. The lights over the desks
and interviewing tables hang down low enough for you to
crack your head. On the walls of corridors is marshalled the
faded past: yellowing prints* once upon a time produced for the
popular inquisitiveness of *Sunday Times* readers; old imaginations
peeling off walls where new ones labour to invent fresh sheets
for mass curiosity. In the editor's office, my first stop, is a full-
sized pop painting with books on one wall and furnishings in red
leather. Instructions have been given to take me to Fleet Street's
El Vino.

---

* Interiors may, of course, have changed in five years. Inevitably many
similar parts of this document are 'history'. To change it all would have
involved a new tour. I hope such preteritions will be minimal and viewed
as secondary to the main body of the work.

On the way my guide, one of Fleet Street's tough and feared men ('I have no emotions whatsoever') casually recalls this story. 'You may not remember, but I used to work for a magazine and one day we sent my wife to interview you. A hatchet job. Let's get at the truth of this man, we thought, he must be a phoney, him and his Centre 42. But she came back saying, "I can't, I can't! He's genuine, talked to me like an equal." It was a good piece, finally.' He's the first of a team of highly intelligent and complex personalities I'm to meet in the course of my researches, a man responsible for unearthing some of the seediest manipulators of our competitive society.

El Vino is full of men without women. No woman is allowed to buy a drink at the bar.* We make for the back where a large, red-streaked-nose man seems to be holding court. He throws open his arms at me and says, 'I want to speak with *that* man.' Thank God my dull brain for names is working. He's a theatre reviewer — lovely man, careless critic. It looks as though wit and anecdotes are about to buzz, but little happens. I'm relieved, the pressure to be funny is always depressing. There's an atmosphere of shabby, besotted agitation where consolations and praises are passed between moist lips; a place where, I feel, reporters tell each other the real truth and share their weariness of the world. I don't know what I'm supposed to feel but attempt to feel it. Soon I'm drunk and trying not to show it. Later we eat spaghetti across the road joined by three other journalists called along by my guide to help him out with his not very forthcoming guest: a literary editor — quiet and retiring as though fearful of being caught too friendly with a literary man; an Eastern European

---

* Despite the Sex Discrimination Act this still operates. Speaking for El Vino after a failed recent attempt to object to their licence being renewed, Mr R. F. Tovey was quoted in *The Times*, March 26th, 1977: 'I hope you can think, as far as the ladies are concerned, that these practices are done in a manner of old world common courtesy and decency and not as a matter of discrimination. If it is discrimination, it is in their favour.'

correspondent, nicely modest and full of questions; and a free-lance who, he reminds me later, had interviewed me for television six years ago and I'd forgotten. He works hard to extinguish my embarrassment.

My guide ends his tour at the Wig and Pen club where, quite drunk, I make some observation which wins his admiration. 'There,' he says, 'I've been with you all day and I've been wondering—what makes this man talented? He's not very witty, a bit reticent—but wham! You come out with an observation like that and I realise—that's his genius.' He confirms my fear that I'm expected to produce instant brilliance and I'm relieved to find I'd accidentally let slip at least one bright remark.

'Journalists write for other journalists, the people they have lunch with rather than the reader. Except for political journalists—they write for politicians. Who knows what the reader wants? One of the reasons newspapers are always running opinion polls is that they don't know what the reader thinks.'

Editorial conference

The atmosphere is casual, relaxed. They wear a mixture of clothing: pink shirts and red ties, smart lawyer suits, pin stripes, sports jackets. It reflects assorted backgrounds. Old hands and young academics; some from provincial papers, others from the rough hustling of defunct popular dailies. Everyone seems to have read all the papers before 9 a.m. and listened to everything on radio and TV. My problem in the beginning is I can't hear what they're saying because I'm so absorbed by the way they're saying it.

'What are we going to do about Bengal this week?'

The editor lifts the internal phone to the sports editor. 'Hello, John? Yesterday's *Financial Times*. Page 12. Second column, three up from the bottom. Aston Villa football club is offering you, me and others shareholdings in the club. Might make a good story for "Inside Track". Who is selling them, how many, why and who's buying? O.K.?' He puts down the receiver and sparkles at a colleague: 'You going to listen to us and put the papers down and stop reading?'

'Yes, when you've stopped phoning.' The conference begins.

'The trouble is we're all in agreement that we're right and they're wrong.'

'Oh, I don't know, I'm more inflationary than you.'

'Are you? Well *you're* wrong then. What about the rest of the government's strategy? I think we're entitled to be absolutely critical of all aspects by now and it would be absolutely consistent with our policy of criticism throughout.'

'There *is* no economic strategy.'

'But there is a philosophy. I mean "let lame ducks go to the wall and stand on your own two feet" *is* a philosophy.'

'Yes, but it's not a strategy.'

'Where are we on Soyuz?'

'No further than any other newspaper.

'I thought the *Daily Mail* did it very well this morning, very well indeed.'

'Maybe, but I didn't like all that science fiction writing.'

'Oh, I thought that was interesting, I liked that. Do we know why the monkey died last time?'

'Boredom, I think.'

'What about the escaped Soviet space scientist?'

'Who's got his head at the moment?'

'Foreign Office, isn't it?'

'Can he be got at?'

'Put in an official request, I think.'

'I think you'd better do that.'

'O.K. I will, although the rumour is that he doesn't know one end of a space craft from another and that in fact he's a ballistics expert.'

The news editor raises the issue of high explosives hidden in the Welsh mountains, he thinks it's a danger and that the local population ought to be told; but apparently the government have slapped a 'D' notice on it and he's told: 'It may be a "D" notice we ought to respect. After all we don't want the other side to know where we keep our bombs and we all know there's a lot of mad Irishmen running around trying to get their hands on some high explosives.'

Confronted with how much news *isn't* used I realise now, if I hadn't realised it before, the amount of news which the media pour out. And I begin wondering to what extent journalists are aware of how they inundate people with information about events which depress and confuse them while not at the same time offering a way out from feelings of impotence. And are they conscious that news has become a marketable commodity to whose 'packaging', like all commodities, special attention must be paid? Do they constantly question themselves, scrutinise their decisions in order to maintain a delicate balance between the demands to decorate the package and the responsibility to present it accurately? Not always easy. Accuracy may be boring, too complex, often bewilderingly contradictory. Contradictions in a complex world must be a difficult commodity to sell.

'Poor Arnold, this must be frustrating for you, not being able to say anything and listening to us pass judgments and decide our opinions in five minutes on major issues. But we've worked together a long time now; what you're hearing is the result of hours spent talking on these issues at other times.' It doesn't help.

'The *Sunday Times*? It's not a newspaper, more an
adventure playground for journalists.'

Amblings

I wander around. People stop and talk to me. I feel intimidated
but don't let it be seen; instead I shamelessly allow my reputation
to go before me. They don't guess that I don't know what I'm
looking for or what questions to ask. The men I meet are fast
thinking, knowledgeable, have firsts from Oxbridge or scars
from searing experiences around the world. And they all exude
that quality of being 'good and honourable men'. But to them
I'm 'the artist', a 'magic man' who can, without actually knowing, see the truth behind the façade, the devil in the making. I
feel them behave in special ways in my presence. My advantage
is doubled: what they suspect are my special powers of perception plus the fact—which I enjoy—that it's they instead of me
who are under scrutiny. My disadvantage is the problem of
disentangling the truth from the performance they're giving.
'That's the problem of the reporter,' I'm told, 'and you're facing
it in the presence of the best performers in the business.' My aim
is to be unobtrusive, shadowy. Occasionally, inspired, I phrase
the right question; mostly, they credit me with having asked the
right question and simply talk. My external demeanour, hope-
fully, is cool and assured. Secretly I'm startled at the speed with
which they grasp the drift of my doubts, confused by the
shorthand language they adopt to communicate ideas among
themselves, and frequently overwhelmed by the incomprehensible technical vocabulary they call upon whether dealing
with economics, diplomatic affairs or our technical times.

We chat in odd corners, on the stairs, in the pub at lunch-time,
and I sense a genuine, disarming eagerness to reveal, justify. 'I
suppose in my field I'm amongst the top three in Fleet Street,'

says one in response to a question from me about his future. I find it an honest, innocent reply. I believe him. But what would he have done with such a statement from me? He'd have gone to town on that one, a juicy quote to reveal the conceit of his victim.

Everyone laughs loudly at his own jokes. 'Have you noticed,' someone asks over lunch, 'how we all flatter each other?' 'No,' I reply, 'but I've noticed how you all *wait* for each other's flattery.' My wit is ignored, which hurts since it's so rare; and he continues. 'I went to play tennis with someone from the business page who'd just investigated Hitachi or some such — I'd never read the business page, who does? — but I did it for that game so that I was able to say between balls: "I didn't think you'd been to Japan last month."'

Their conversation is rapid and their laughter covers the common ground of mutually recognised foibles or the in-tales of other Fleet Street journalists. 'Wilson said of her or was it Crossman?: "Political journalist? That bitch would get a scoop wrong if you gave it to her at dictation speed."' I have difficulty in stretching my smile to cover all their funnies, a great many of which are delivered in the shorthand of a shared working experience that's unfamiliar to me. I'm told, and must remember, that when in editorial conferences they argue for space and seem not to be taking anything seriously, it's because they have to represent their story in caricature terms in order not to be caught being serious, which would be an invitation to derision. Seriousness, they assure me, appears while they're discussing and canvassing for support in the corridors — as with any establishment possessing power. Why does seriousness invite derision? Pomposity, yes. Is that what is meant? Do journalists have difficulty in being serious without being pompous?

I experience, then, their desperate need to be found witty — a highly prized and regarded attribute, demonstrating, I suppose, the cool detachment they feel is required for the sober assessment of news. Or is it that immured in what they see as the ghastly spectacle world news presents of man's stupidity and inhumanity they're forced to develop wit as a safety valve? Whatever, it's not easy to sustain an appreciative grin for a whole day, every day, and I can never be quite certain whether the wit is a safety valve against the world's horrors or against suspicions of their impotence to do anything about them.

One of the issues agitating them in my first week is the publication of Eysenck's book, *Race, Intelligence and Education*. Everyone wants to attack it. 'I mean look at this paragraph: "Nearly every anatomical, physiological and bio-chemical system investigated shows racial differences. Why should the brain be an exception?" Well,' they explode, 'why *shouldn't* it? *Nearly* every system shows racial differences, he says. Well, if *not* "every" why not make a point of *that*? And if "*nearly* every" then how can he ask "why should the brain be an exception?" It's such unscientific thinking and writing that makes me so suspicious of the man.'

I read a transcript of a conversation three journalists have had with Eysenck. One of the questions asked is: 'Could you be accused of erring according to Liam Hudson's law of selective attention to data?' It seems an odd question to be asked by a journalist whose profession is entirely given to just that, selecting data. 'Public figures are in danger of complacency,' says one journalist, 'so need to be continually liable to attack. The hunting pleasure, though I don't approve of it, is one of the satisfactions of journalism.'

But not only does the journalist's work appear every day multiplying the law of 'selective attention to data', he also seems to assume his individual power is minimal without taking into account the power residing in the *totality* of the press. Who curbs the greater sense of complacency that must come from that?

Who will hunt, probe and attack the strange motives *he* may have?

> 'The journalist claims and exercises the moral right
> to expose other individuals whose moral
> righteousness they suspect.'

Insight

It's a strange name to give a column. What can it mean? In-depth? Probe? Mystical illumination? The word suggests a virtue usually claimed by literature which has time to explore contradictions and paradoxes and be subtly perceptive about them. Can a newspaper do and be these things?

Their office has a large print of Mao on the wall and a poster saying: 'Women of Britain say — GO! 1920', rather like photographs of nudes which boys hang in their rooms at public school to assert their independence while temporarily trapped by the enemy. But I'm assured that's not the case: 'I bought it as a pure piece of art — the design of propaganda art interests me deeply.' Everyone is young, surely under thirty, and seems to care.

Insight, I'm told, has created journalistic history: the detailed and complicated investigative reporting of issues and scandals of a public, social and political nature, a procedure 'often involving confrontation with very difficult people'. Normally a newspaper is laid out on the basis of a number of assumptions: a) the reader's intellectual limitations — big print, short, snappy articles, a photographic profusion of breasts, thighs, action; b) the reader's sexual appetites and voyeuristic inclinations — cover the law courts for cases of rape, adultery, vicarage orgies; c) intellectual aspirations — wide arts coverage, diaries of politicians, international news concerning industrial development;

d) the place where the paper is likely to be read – in a train to and from work, at leisure by the breakfast teapot, in the lounge on a Sunday morning, and so on. But until the advent of Insight it seemed that every newspaper, from the so-called pops to the so-called heavies, agreed that (wherever they individually gauged it) all newspaper readers did have a saturation point, a kind of text sound-barrier beyond which print dizziness set in or the reader went berserk. In the *News of the World* it may have been a whole page relieved by many photographs and in the *Observer* it may have been a whole page stubbornly stripped of photographs, but no one, it was felt, had patience or powers of concentration for more.

Insight thought differently: if the issue was important enough and if they spent more than the normal time which a trip, a chat and a bit of back-number reading involved, then there would be an intelligent readership for it. More, they were also prepared to spend the money to prove it, and did.

At my request they recite their record:

'The RB211 fiasco, how it happened and what the various governments were doing. Scandals in local government contracting. The failures in air safety regulations which led to the deaths of 72 people, unnecessarily, after their aircraft crashed and caught fire at Rijeka. Then a long account of the effects of a restrictive abortion policy in Birmingham which, because senior doctors in the area disapproved, led to disastrous medical decisions such as refusing to abort German measles babies. Then a long and sympathetic analysis of Wilson's efforts to hold Labour together over the E.E.C., by far the most detailed, and kindest, to appear. Then Northern Ireland, internment, we moved over there and remained for almost a year involved in much patient and occasionally risky work, confronting massed public opinion ... '

It's impressive. Some people find their tone self-righteous, and confronting them is a bit like walking towards a policeman – the knowledge of his function makes you feel guilty for something or other. But they seem to have no pretensions about being authorities on the world and if their articles finally give the impression that they've become instant experts on everything, this is a result more of the unavoidably persuasive power of print and less a reflection of their own delusions.

In my week with them they are investigating falling bridges but, it seems, with scant enthusiasm. 'This subject must have priority over something, though God knows what!' The impression of indifference is a false one, the result of a strange journalistic disease they call 'hyping' (from the Greek word *huperbole* which first came into the English language in about 1529 and means 'exaggeration'). Behind the shorthand of jokes and the contrived casualness is the reading, they tell me, of a lot of technical reports, innumerable consultations with construction experts and midnight meetings between themselves and *Sunday Times* technical experts.

I don't see any of this. It takes place in other rooms and at other hours. What I see are four people on the telephone at once; it's difficult to follow all their conversations but it's obvious that at this stage they don't know anything about their subject. With disarming honesty they phone around for enlightenment.

'Professor Wells in Belfast, please ... Professor Wells? Ah, good morning, Insight *Sunday Times* here. Look, I don't know how to start thinking on this subject at all – yes, the fallen bridges, you've guessed it – I don't know what are the questions to ask nor in what order nor who can answer them or how you set them up. Can I ring you again when I've worked out some basic shape to the piece and ask you whether it makes engineering sense?'

Another member of the team is making a brave attempt to understand, he's on to a ministry official.

'I'm very much a layman so if I could explain in layman's language rather than your usual language of expertise ... but as I understand it, it goes something like this: I build shelves for 15lb jam jars, test the shelves by putting 20lb jam jars on, use 15lb jam jars for 20 years and then return to 20lb jam jars ... Oh! I see. Jam jars are hardly applicable. Of course. Well, let's start again ... '

They nurse each other's incomprehensions.

'As far as I can make out it's a perfectly decent feat of engineering but no one seems to have taken account of the fact that the things are built by incompetent, lumpen Irish labourers who don't give a damn.'

Someone tells me an Insight anecdote:

'You know, the Conservative Party thinks the *Sunday Times* is Maoist and *The Times* merely left wing. I was talking to this woman, Mrs O, and she whispered to me: "I think you've got three full card paying members of the Communist Party on your Insight team." And I said to her, "Oh no! They're not as right wing as that".'

A bottle of wine arrives. The People column have sent it. It seems departments send gifts to staff colleagues who supply them with a story. People gives wine, Atticus gives whisky.

Loyalties to sources of information present problems for journalists. Insight investigated the collapse of the Vehicle & General Insurance Company and found from a high-ranking contact in the Board of Trade that they'd known about the company's precarious condition but had received directives from the government not to enquire further, as the Tories were pursuing a 'hands off industry' policy. At the tribunal investigating the V. & G.'s collapse, the reporter was called as a witness and asked to reveal his source of information. He refused, which left the tribunal able to dismiss his evidence as mere hearsay, thus undermining the impact of the *Sunday Times*'s investigation. They also have to grapple with the law of slander which prevents a reporter asking a question designed to find out if unsavoury assertions are true; a double-edged law which helps the citizen protect his private life and hampers the journalist who wishes to expose it to view – a good thing; or put another way: a law which helps the swindler to keep his activities secret and hampers the journalist who wants to expose it – a bad thing.

My interpretation of this law becomes a corner-stone in a stern conflict which arises between Insight and myself. When an early draft of this *Journey* appears some of the team are very distressed to find I've written anything at all about my stay at the *Sunday Times* and their reactions range from irritation at certain facts I've got wrong or omitted, to courteous fury that I'd set out to create, as they see it, an image of 'shallow-minded shits – who make fools of themselves on complex matters of genuine public concern such as unsafe bridges ... '

Basically the protests come from three quarters: Insight themselves are mainly concerned that I've got facts wrong in a way which cruelly misrepresents their function:

'Does the sort of brutal, vulgar approach you present – and it is just that – really sort with our record?'

One of the managing editors who had been closely associated with Insight is upset by the overall image, and imagines I'd only ever intended to write this diary and therefore claimed their attention under false pretences:

'Did you really think that because you managed to prevail upon Harry's generosity, that this gave you a licence to say what you like about anyone employed by the *Sunday Times*? Do you really think that when a man goes to work for a company, that he surrenders his reputation into their hands? I find it hard to be quite sure what your moral stance was in your negotiations with the editor. You seem to have been a bit sinuous ... '

Another journalist, who has been very helpful to me in discussing the problems of the play, feels I've misrepresented the *Sunday Times*, been inaccurate in reporting editorial conferences and, like his colleague, feels I've been devious:

'You make everyone out to be ruthless, ambitious, clever and cynical about the stuff they are dealing with. That may be true of a few people. But it misses out large numbers of reporters and other writers who are unruthless to the point of inertia, who do not spend their life making wittily flip remarks about anything that comes their way, and who do not possess that self-deprecatory arrogance which emerges from a lot of the voices you report. A lot of people here are very ordinary people doing reasonably well the only job they are capable of doing at all. Far from parading their self-confidence in the way you suggest, they are conscious of working low down in a vast capitalist organisation. They are intensely self-critical both about the paper and about their own efforts — a point which emerges not at all from your account, yet which is fundamental to the paper's vitality ... '

I spend days going over my draft to see if they're right and write long letters of defence. Yes, I have made some mistakes; no, I haven't made everyone out to be cynical — they're too touchy on that point — but, most important, I get furious at their suggestions of deviousness. Fortunately I've carefully filed all correspondence so it can be proved I've wanted, from the start, to send the piece to everyone for approval. It takes massive and angry letters lumbering back and forth to get them to acknowledge this. Seven pages of quarto size from one ends: ' ... You may find the tone of this letter a little sharp from time to time: however I've refrigerated my original feelings as far as possible ... ' I reply with eight and a half foolscap pages: ' ... I wish you'd have placed some of your sanctimony into the freezer along with your hot passions and spared me both ... '

The confusion grows. Someone from the *Sunday Times* anonymously sends a dossier to *Private Eye*, who ring me up for confirmation of 'suppression'. I tell them no, I've just got some facts wrong and certain people are questioning them. As usual *they* get it wrong (calling me, among other mistakes, Hampstead's leading playwright when in fact I'm Highgate's) and I'm compelled to write what they call 'Long Boring Letter' in order to set certain facts right. In the process I quote without mentioning names, an extract from one of the angry letters to me, which act arouses further and greater anger. I seem not to be doing anything right.

But the encounter is interesting in that it produces the journalistic paranoia about which many people have spoken to me, and in that I'm forced to concede and correct mistakes and to face the curious fact that people I'd liked and a column I'd respected emerges, in my early draft, as a very thin etching indeed. It's worth going into detail.

My original draft relies on observation. I *hear* them making jokes about fallen bridges—I don't *see* them ploughing through reports. I *hear* them phoning around for information—I don't *see* them in consultation with technical advisers. What I get from these observations, and think my original draft is communicating with approval, is the sober and responsible way the team are tackling the story. I write: ' ... it's obvious they don't know anything about their subject. With disarming honesty they phone around for enlightenment ... ', and it seems to me I'm pointing to a laudable quality: modesty. Look, I'm saying, they have no pretensions, they don't delude themselves that they are instant experts on bridge building but begin by admitting they know nothing and start from there. Why, after all, *should* they be experts on the world? No! they write to me: ' ... what emerges is that Insight is a technically sloppy ... group of half-wits ... '

It startles me at first and I'm initially hurt to be so misunder-stood—especially when I'd attempted to write well of them; but on reflection I recognise that their reputation for efficient and accurate investigation is more important to them than a reputa-tion for modest investigation. So, I add to the text, write about 'hyping' and refer to the behind-the-scenes read-throughs of heavy technical jargon with which they struggle.

But a more damaging and complex piece of misreporting seems to be my description of 'the gynaecologist affair'. My first day's guide is determined to put on a 'show' for me and I confess I see more of the show than the facts. Their calm mood has been surprising me but I'm assured that such sweet and quiet atmos-pheres as that hovering around the subdued investigation of tragic fallen bridges are not the rule. They even apologise that there's no story around to enable me to see them in real action. What *can* such action be? I'm soon to find out. Within hours they and their situation change. The show begins.

On Friday afternoon, at 3.30, twenty-four hours before the paper needs to be put to bed, my first day's guide comes in to ask the team if they can handle the story of a National Health Service gynaecologist who has refused a 12-year-old an abortion. She is reported as having said to the child: 'If you play adult games you must expect adult consequences.' A story had been written by a freelance who had structured her copy with a serious tone specially for the *Sunday Times*. She'd offered it to the news desk, who were not all that interested, certainly not at the fee she wanted. She could have got £300 from the *News of the World* but was horrified at the way they wanted to handle it so she came back to the *Sunday Times*, one of whose other more senior editors (my guide) had got hold of it and was now lunging around demanding why the hell the story hadn't been picked up before.

But Insight are reluctant to handle it because they think it's simply another news story. The senior editor disagrees and points out that the gynaecologist is a National Health medical officer, and paid to *help* wayward and confused children of 12, not to pass moral judgments on them. 'Problem is,' he says, 'she's clamped down, refuses to speak to the press. What we want is the story of a guilty gynaecologist. Was she married? Did she have an unhappy love affair? Get a photograph, even if it's of her peering reluctantly round the door.'

'Jesus!' Insight's editor protests, 'that's Harold Robbins, not journalism.'

The team can see that, though there's genuine concern behind the attempt to galvanise them, nevertheless a special performance is being laid on for my benefit and they're slightly embarrassed by it. But they remain loyal, though not without protest. Another of the team insists: 'It's not an Insight story at all, just a classic newsroom story. Girls of 12, even 10 are having abortions all the time.' At this stage activity heightens. Phones slam, a news reporter is brought in. The original story is photostated and handed around. Everyone is briefed.

'You can get up to Bradford in two and a half hours on the M.1.'

'Three and a half.'

'Four.' Suddenly it *seems* like Hollywood journalism in place of the sober assembling of news and opinion I've witnessed till now. And my first draft leaves that impression.

They protest:

'The idea that the *Sunday Times* heavy mob went boiling up
the Motorway that night to rip all the veils from the gynaecologist's psycho-social history within 24 hours is both untrue
and preposterous ... '

Watching them make their plans (even though not ones for
'boiling up the Motorway'), a thought crosses my mind: an
unsuspecting professional citizen, culpable no doubt, is being
gunned for. The hounds are being unleashed, I think; horses are
mounted, blood is smelt, someone has blown the horn. I'm in a
position to telephone her, warn her to put herself, her friends and
her colleagues on guard, to go on holiday, underground. She
may have behaved inhumanly but, so it seems, an inhuman hunt
is on. My pity is aroused and conflicts with the condemnation
I feel for her behaviour. Insight protest again at the way I word
this. They're right. I've been mesmerised by what appears to be
the coming alive of a myth in front of my eyes: the Newspaper
Hunt. 'Basically,' calls out one reporter from the other side of the
room to their galvaniser, 'what you want is all the dirt we can
get on the woman?' 'Yes,' he replies. I scribble my notes: ' ... all
the dirt we can get on the woman ... ' Great copy! And it ties in
with those questions: ' ... was she married? Did she have an
unhappy love affair? ... ' My early draft is full of such wide-eyed
discovery. But the 'hype'! the 'hype'! I'd not known about the
'hype'. The team educate me:

'It's another example of the shorthand that comes from long
proximity that you didn't grasp ... "getting the dirt" didn't
mean getting information about her sex life but her professional record ... '

I next write about the moral implications of pursuing the gynaecologist after the affair is over but I make the mistake of doing so
without asking further questions. There's great confusion. *They*

think I've accused them of a callous indifference to the possibility
of again distressing the mother and child by boiling up the M.1.
to question them; it *could* have been read like that and, since they
are suspicious of the circumstances surrounding the diary's
creation and ill-disposed towards its final shape, they did! But
actually I only mean to suggest that it's the reappearance of the
issue in the press which will again upset them. In a letter explain-
ing this I add what I believe to be a humorous aside: 'What *is*
laughable, of course, is my assumption that mother or daughter
or any friend who might recognise the case would read the
Sunday Times.' My sociological observation is pounced upon as
'just a zany sneer presumably meant to show that no warm, real
working class people would ever read the *Sunday Times*'.

It becomes one of those situations where everything I write is
now misunderstood. The tone of attack and defence grows in
acrimony but I make a great effort not to lose sight of the fact
that I have made mistakes — the main one being my failure to
check that in fact it was the mother herself who had asked a
journalist to investigate the gynaecologist's behaviour; nor did I
notice in the final article that no mention was made of the
mother or child's name. In this way, through inexperience, I
learn how, despite being around for weeks, it's easy to get a
story wrong. (What of the reporter who pops in and out of a
story for a few hours?)

But what I find bewildering is the vehemence of personal
accusation and abuse, most of which is angrily founded upon the
insufficiently investigated assumption that I'd deliberately tried
to get the diary published behind their backs — and this from
people who were accusing me of insufficient investigation!

It depresses me. The onslaught seriously makes me think my
entire first *Journey into Journalism* must be abortive. Everyone
advises me to give up — 'you'll never get it right, they'll always
find something wrong with it.' I spend hours puzzling over

one piece of sinister evidence which, it is thought, proves that I'm ' ... already manipulating the moral environment so that the forthcoming drama will make sense ... ' And what is it? My interpretation of the law of slander – the 'corner-stone' to this conflict. As follows:

I'd written about the difficulty journalists have in grappling with the law of slander which, I wrote, 'prevents the reporter asking a question designed to find out if unsavoury assertions are true'. I imagined myself to be sympathetic to the journalist's problem and continued (it's a fascinating detail, this): ' ... a double-edged law which helps the citizen to protect his private life but hampers the journalist in pursuit of a swindler.'

After telling me this is a sign that I'm 'manipulating the moral environment' my accuser attempts to explain how the law really works. It had taken me a great deal of time to unravel it in the first place, now I'm in even greater confusion. All I can do is simply confess that I don't understand and rebut the accusation of sinister intent. A reply comes back again:

' ... you're going to say I'm patronising. I can't help that if you give the appearance of being stupider than I think you are ... to labour this, the proposition can read, *either*:
A law which helps the citizen protect his private life, AND hampers the journalist who wishes to expose it to view, *or*:
A law which helps the swindler to keep his activities secret, AND hampers the journalist who wants to expose it. The slander law, in other words, doesn't have anything to do with the concept of *privacy* as such, and isn't "double-edged" in the sense you imply.'

It's true – I *am* stupid. I stare and stare at the two propositions. Surely if one can apply 'either' proposition then that makes the law double-edged? The law protects the citizen's private life, which is a good thing, but protects the swindler's activity, which is a bad thing – and which is what I'd written originally! I want to give up, but my accuser returns with further explanations:

'Put it this way: suppose Lord A has a mistress – a true fact which he rightly regards as private. Mr B from the *Daily Sneer* goes to Lord A's neighbour, Lady C, who does not know about the mistress, and says: "Did you know that your neighbour Lord B keeps a mistress? Do you think that he ought to be cut by the County?" There is no way in which the law of slander would help the unfortunate Lord B protect his private life, since all defamation law works on the principle that you can say what the hell you like about anyone, provided it can be proven true. (Let's assume that Mr B has a picture of the mistress' backside with Lord A's fingerprints on it.)

As it happens, the difficulty about slanderous questions usually arises not with the simple questions that unpleasant gossip-columnists want to ask about people's private lives. (Which anyway aren't usually defamatory: has Belinda Blackstrap got married? Has Arnold Wesker, the famous playwright, moved from Highgate to Hampstead?) The difficulty arises when you are trying to find out whether last year's profit and loss account contained items that should have gone into the capital account (i.e. are they fiddling the profit figures before flogging the business off) and the like. My objection to your false apposition was, and is, that it suggests that the choice society has to make is between more financial investigation, and therefore more personal prying, or less financial investigation and therefore less prying.

Whether we are going to see eye to eye on this I just don't know. But anyway, I think you must put in either more, or nothing of this.'

I have put in more!

There is one curious objection which I cannot understand: a paragraph near the end of *Journey* reads:

'I'm asked if I've found out where the power lies in the newspaper. It's an innocent question which suddenly brings into focus the submerged patterns of fighting egos. I don't envy the Captain who has to control this team of brilliantly intimidating social terrorists.'

The objection is strongly felt:

'I dislike your piece chiefly because it calls me a social terrorist (among, by implication, other things). I think that it is (a) untrue and (b) insulting. And I take it seriously because I don't have the faintest sympathy with the sweet English idea that journalism, politics and public affairs generally should be a jovial exchange of custard pies, after which everyone wipes their chops and shakes hands.'

It comes as a surprise to me that such a sweet English idea exists but I insist on retaining the description which, when the words 'brilliantly intimidating' are added to 'social terrorists' and the whole is set in context, is an obviously affectionate one.

But all that's irrelevant. Why, I ask myself, is there such an acrimoniously distorted reading of my long document at all? Why haven't they said: 'Look, you've got some things seriously wrong, let's go through it and see if we can get a more accurate story without interfering with your opinion of us'? Some had done it, even Insight's editor came around to doing it, but ... not others ...

Still, keeping my fingers crossed that the acrimony will die down, I rewrite this section, the doing of which teaches me about the traps and pitfalls of investigatory journalism into which I've fallen and produces from them some valuable comments on its problems. It only niggles me somewhat that I didn't get all this as a result of perspicacious questioning on my part but had to blunder and evince it in anger. Nevertheless the comments are dramatic and, because deeply felt, sympathetic.

'Your main question is what material would have been denied you if everyone had known that your intention was to publish a piece about the *Sunday Times*. If the editor had approved that project, I suppose that a number of people would have spoken to you, but probably after first attempting to persuade the editor that there was neither duty nor a merit in opening our door to any outside writer. If the editor had stuck to his view, then doubtless some people would have co-operated. But in general I think that whatever warmth and expansiveness you managed to generate as a seeker after good lines and good atmosphere for a play would have been much diminished if your purpose had been different ... I would not have agreed to your coming to any editorial conferences. Even a proper journalist would find it extremely difficult to convey accurately how policy is made at the *Sunday Times*, or any other paper. I am afraid your own effort quite fails to do it justice ... But even if you had been able to take a complete tape-recording, and added your interpretative comments, I don't see why I should be in favour of it being published. Is a Cabinet in favour of its meetings being publicised? Is there any reason why a newspaper, if it takes itself seriously, should be any more favourably disposed? If newspapers can get hold of Cabinet minutes or the gist of Cabinet discussions, they will doubtless use them. But that does not mean that Cabinet Ministers have the faintest obligation to surrender these things. if that is not in their interest. Similarly, I can't see that we have the smallest obligation to agree to your publishing our private conversations ... '

In all fairness it must be added that not everyone agreed:

'... nothing strikes me as being so offensive/inaccurate/un-
acceptable as to rule out publication ... ' and ' ... Naturally I
disagree cordially with large portions of it; but I must fight to
the death for your right to publish it, damned or otherwise.
Actually I enjoyed it very much, though I think you missed
several quite important facets of our being (perhaps because
we were all so busy making five-layer jokes about them). On
balance though I rather deplore the fact that we are not
publishing it ourselves ... ' and ' ... For God's sake how
embarrassing and wrong that people here should object to
what you write, and should make threatening legal noises.
That seems to me monstrous, however inaccurate, unfair or
damaging they may think your book is. If we do that kind of
thing what right have we to go on writing about others? It
should be, I think, an absolute principle that we should let
others do unto us what we do unto others. Or we should give
up altogether ... '

Finally, Insight's defence of itself:

'... We not only made no mention of the gynaecologist's
personal life, love life, etc., we in fact undertook no enquiries
to find out anything about that side of things. Certainly we
inquired about her professional record — what did her colleagues etc. think might explain the decision, e.g. was she
Catholic; had she had a gruelling time with abortion requests;
any one of a number of things like that which might explain
her attitude. Because we found no particularly outstanding
personal beliefs, etc., we said nothing about her as a person at
all — presenting a very flatly written story simply about the
conflict between a child and a doctor; and leaving the reader
to side with whoever they wished. That may not be art, and it
has its massive limitations. But it certainly is not the sort of
brutalising, gutter approach that you credit us with ... You

misunderstood a) the degree to which X was acting and b) the private language "guilty gynaecologist" ... It's another example of the shorthand that comes from long proximity that you didn't grasp. (This particular joke relates to a comment from Murray Sayle once: "There are only two types of story: We Name the Guilty Man. And: Arrow Points To The Defective Part.") Which tells you a lot about popular journalism, and expresses a basic truth ... This failure to see our work in the round comes out most clearly in your description of the inquiry into bridges. If we described a week's work by listening to the first 15 minutes and then selecting that – plus a few jokes – as representative of the whole, you would be rightly appalled. Yet that is precisely what you have done. Did you know the work we put into that? Did you look at the technical reports we ploughed through, ask what construction experts we had consulted, record any of the long and detailed meetings we held among ourselves and with long-standing technical assistants on this? No ... Of course, agreed, the power of Insight is frightening, because irresponsible in the real sense of the word.* Hence the almost self-righteous effort to define all the time what one *is* responsible to, what one is trying to do ... who are we to impinge upon people's lives? (Yet most of the time they are powerful men, not helpless Mrs Jones.) What do we hope to find? The truth? But if that is locked away in the private motives, doubts, hesitancies only half recognised even by the principals in any story, how can outsiders hope to understand? ... But much of your view of the paper – Insight included – was blurred by the difficulties of adjusting stereotypes to reality. Because so many newspapermen really do see themselves in the fast talking, "Get the story, kid" Ben Hect mould – newspapermen as a breed being in reality insecure and prone to cardigans and commuting, but

* Meaning 'power without responsibility'.

cherishing dreams of themselves fed mainly by Warner Brothers (*and* don't believe that the *Guardian* are any different). But newspapers don't really work like that. Only the surface is terribly convincing – so many people want to make it so. The *Sunday Times* has the added disadvantage, from the outsider's point of view, that the element of parody is perhaps stronger here than elsewhere; yet the surface we do adopt and would call our own – which your editorial conference catches cleverly – is equally phoney ... There are great limitations to the Insight technique. The Ulster book is a compendium of them, as a perceptive review by Roy Hattersley, the ex-Labour Minister in charge of the Army in Ulster in Wilsons' Government, pointed out. The limitations of narrative form as a vehicle for analysis; the limitations of deducing motive from action; the danger that post hoc becomes inevitably propter hoc in a narrative relying upon sequence; the imposition upon a reader, the arrogant demand (unless we are careful) that he trusts us, imposed by the protection of sources; the argument over what we are trying to portray ... all these are valid problems ... we don't give a damn whether we emerge "unblemished heroes and champions of justice", so long as we are at least excoriated for genuine failings ... '

'Journalism is the task of blaming other people while diverting blame from yourself. That's why good journalists tend to be paranoid.'

The leader conferences

'I want to ask John to do something on women being barred from the Stock Exchange.'*

* Shortly after this, a ruling was passed to allow women into the Stock Exchange.

'Quite right. You can't claim to be a fabric of the national economy and then claim the privileges of a private club.'

'I was thinking of a light-hearted leader, not an occasion for solemnity.'

'Of course not. They're making such fools of themselves.'

'They say it's because they wouldn't be able to tell dirty jokes on the floor.'

'But John's on the Persian Gulf. Peter?'

'How long is the Persian Gulf?'

'About 300.'

'Good, that leaves me about 400 to do the Stock Exchange.'

'Do you want the leader on the Persian Gulf to have a message? A punch line?'

'Yes, start with that joke about the Arabs.'

'Which one?'

'Oh, that one about—how does it go? Showing they can't ever agree on anything. Do you have time to do it?'

'Good lor, yes. I'll do it tonight.'

'Soyuz? A leader on that?'

'I'd much sooner do Soyuz than the Mafia. I don't believe the Mafia exists.'

'What could we do on it?'

'Oh, I thought we could tackle "What's the point of it all, is it worth it, isn't this a right moment to get together?" '

'By the way, let's get Godfrey to go through all the Pentagon papers and select what he wants and ask what space he wants in an ideal world then tell him it's not an ideal world.'

On the one hand they communicate a sense of immediate action, despite the flippant tone, as though the world will, tomorrow, be changed, informed, surprised. It's exciting. Here lies power. And if not action then certainly activity. On the other hand they also communicate the ease and confidence of living in a cocoon. Like actors in a company as opposed to freelance

actors. Their fields of responsibility are defined, as are the limits
to which they need exercise that responsibility. They have a job,
known, palpable, for which they have established patterns and
precedents every week of the past.

> 'I write letters of resignation every year ... a
> journalist is only ever a man of the times. Personally
> as an academic, I find I'm involved in a great conflict
> between journalism's demands of superficiality and
> my own training in academic precision. Sometimes
> I think I'm in journalism simply because I'm unfit for work.'

But a leader conference is considered to be the paper's palpitating
heart. There was great concern lest I missed them. I said I'd been
to one and was told one was not enough. 'You've no idea what
heart-searchings go on here over the leaders. We spend hours
discussing issues. And the differences of opinion we have! Ha!
And the way we reconcile them! We're always having conflicts,
changing each other's mind. I'm always changing my mind, I
can always be persuaded. Don't believe strength is such a great
virtue. Compassion is much more important. That gynaecologist
story — you didn't hear the quarrel we had over *that* one ...'

So, sometime later, I sit in on another leader conference. Only
three people present. Mostly there's five or six. Representing
university and brilliant youth is a heavy-limbed and kindly faced
man looking like the brother you've always wanted at your side
to be commonsensical, tender and firm. Then, immaculately
dressed — thank God! — is the kind of man with age deceptive,
charm lethal, and fair good looks reassuring, representing
journalism's ambassador to the elegant dining rooms of influence,
wit and adequate conversation. And finally, with alertness to
danger pouring out of every finely tuned intelligent glance and
movement — the captain: a cheeky, thoroughbred working-class

mongrel about whom I guess that, coming from an under-privileged background, he'd made bloody sure there was no part of the operation he couldn't do himself. (And I shall call them just that: Brother, Ambassador and Captain.)

The Captain begins: 'We're rather stuck this week.'

The Brother picks up: 'Oh, I don't know. There's that piece you suggested on the Stockholm conference. All that traffic congestion due to a conference on environment! Nice irony. I'd like to do something on that. Link it up to Peyton's statement. Did you read it? It's quite staggering actually –'

'Yes,' says the Captain, 'I'm surprised the dailies didn't pick that one up.' The Ambassador asks, what.

'Well,' continues the Brother, 'there's all these hundreds of delegates, all meeting under the United Nations banner, with our own Minister of Environment, Walker, as one of them; and here's Peyton, a junior minister of transport *under* Walker making this incredible statement in the House about *not* putting certain regulations into force, which had been agreed on in the House last year, remember? Regulations about reducing the noise from cars by three or four decibels? And why not? Because he'd been under pressure from the car industry who were complaining that it would have forced them into higher costs and reduced their competitiveness in the Common Market. And Peyton says that as the motor industry is of such importance to the country –'

Captain: 'That's just the sort of detail we should be following up. I'm tired of all these end-of-the-world stories when in fact there are hundreds of small problems which *can* be attended to – like the sulphur content of the air.'

Brother: 'Just what politicians are good at if they're good at anything. Little things like that, cleaning the Thames or the London air, and it works.'

Captain: 'Oh, I'm not complacent about the air of London.

They say it'll come back, smog; something to do with the
effect of sunlight on the fumes.'

The discussion is disjointed. Everyone throwing facts and
observations into a common pool from which the shape of the
leaders might emerge.

Brother: 'I mean, look at Rio Tinto Zinc ploughing up North
Wales. They found nothing and went off somewhere else. All
that promise of work to the local community.'

Ambassador: 'But if this club of Rome, or whatever it's called,
is right and we only have copper for the next 25 years then I
should think we ought to plough up the whole of North Wales.
After all we're only a small manufacturing country —'

Captain: '*I* should think the answer is to find a substitute for
copper.'

Ambassador: 'Is there one?'

Brother: 'And then there's Crossman's argument that it's all
very well for you middle-class people to start getting upset about
pollution and the environment but it all comes from what
increases the standards of living of the working class.'

Captain: '*Is* that true? Anyone gone into that? Actually
worked it out? I mean away with lead in petrol! Away with
sulphur in coal! Down with noise! Fine! But does it really lead
to anti-growth?'

The Captain then tells a story of how when he was editor an
attack from the *Northern Echo* on a certain industrial practice by
ICI led to ICI modifying some piping system which in turn
led to increased demands for lead piping. '*That* wasn't anti-
growth, that was stimulation.' It's a good story but the
Ambassador gently suggests it's a special case and can't really
prove a principle.

The early part of the discussion is a kind of 'feeling' session.
Tentative. Issues aren't discussed right through, they're dropped
and picked up again later. The Captain brings up the railways

dispute. Should they do anything on that? It's sniffed at, pawed and passed by. Stockholm engages them more for the moment.

The Captain returns to the Crossman thesis and asks, 'Have we countered it?' Pollution (quality of living) versus wages (material standards of living). 'I mean, supposing we said all cars should be kept out of the city centres, would this reduce the need for cars, cut down on production jobs?' They agree that it's details like that which need to be followed through. 'I mean,' continues Captain, 'there's a brilliant article in the *Standard*. Anyone read it? About pulling down Soho and what it meant in terms of destroying a community. Absolutely first-rate stuff, I thought, showing a proper concern for human beings and history and atmosphere. *That's* the kind of approach we should be making. We need to stay off the cosmic level and stick to specifics.'

At once my sympathies go soaring. I want to applaud. (And when the paper comes out on the following Sunday there's an article on the Stockholm conference – 'Why the poor always lose' – pursuing the Crossman theme.) But after the initial silent leap of joy the old ambivalence sets in. Why do they merely tinker with such enormous problems? Why do they scatter and dissipate attention instead of focusing it? They seem to be hovering on the edge of something to be grabbed at as a fundamental theme: the Captain's question: what would happen if all city centres were cleared of cars? Whom would it affect? Not only the car industry's management but also the industry's workers; and from them – the unions; then the pedestrian, who might benefit from the increased safety and fresh air, or is it likely that shopkeepers would suffer because fewer people would come into town? Or would *more* people come? They might, if the public transport system were more effective. And what about free fares during rush hours? And the effects on motor insurance; the decline in revenue from motor tax? And what else? The ageless theme of interdependence. Why didn't they go into it in a big way? Surely such a debate contained many features of those other problems flooding our approach to the year 2000?

I think to myself: if I edited a newspaper I'd make the leader its raison d'être. If an issue is worth drawing attention to then attention should be drawn to it by onslaught. There are so many questions to ask, so many aspects to consider. Is it seriously considered that an issue is dignified simply by being given a wider column beneath a regal escutcheon? Surely nothing can disguise the little bits of pontification which go thumping down one third of the 'Opinion' page?

A new subject is thrown into the melting pot: the Ambassador thinks the recent bid by France for political leadership of Europe is worthy of a leader. 'I mean, Pompidou's attitude is a bit like the trade unions: "we'll negotiate providing you come to the table with an already packaged and acceptable offer." What does "negotiate" mean? Did you read it this morning? The French want to shift the headquarters for the political secretariat from Brussels to Paris, and they're insisting on French being the official language. It's all obviously a bid for political leadership of Europe and I think we should stand up against it.'

The Captain asks if he's against spreading the pleasures of the French language? 'Indeed not,' says the Ambassador, 'as a lover of it myself—no! By all means. But facts are facts, it *is* a minority language and I don't see the sense of spending a lot of money on publicity to promote it.'

They return to the impending railway strike. 'I'm afraid I'm an appeasement man,' says the Ambassador. 'I mean, tell me, someone, one of you who is a "strength" man, what is hoped will happen by the government remaining firm? Who will it teach a good lesson to, to bring the railway to a halt? Will it establish a principle? And let's forget the precedent of the miners—if that's possible. Is the cost of disruption worth it? Captain, what do you think?'

'I've been trying to work out what I think all bloody week.' There's a discussion about the percentages and no one can agree on exactly what is being asked or what is being offered. Is Business News doing anything on it? The editor of Business News is called up (and we'll call him the Business Man).

Now something very strange happens. The Captain says: 'Of course, the left feels that the unions must extract all they can get.' Someone says, 'that's anarchy,' and someone questions who the hell the left is. There is a pause.

'Trouble is,' says the Brother, 'the unions used to know what was on and what wasn't on; now they look at a wage packet and ask is it worth striking for anything but a large increase.' There's another pause.

Someone says, 'And I think there's a tendency to see it as a much larger struggle within competitive society.' Pause, yet again, slightly longer.

'The "them and us" struggle is really on,' says the Ambassador. The pause lengthens, like a train of thought grinding to a halt under threat.

Someone says, 'And it doesn't help when they can see such enormous profits being made in property.' They have paused – utterly.

I sense a profound reflection. Again they seem on the edge of a major debate. Brother touched on it: the actual size of the wage packet. It has always seemed manifest lunacy to me that workers are expected to be happy, civilised, fulfilled and unfearful of the future, doing the work they do for the wages they receive. Today's society is one in which the teacher is scorned as scant investment by bank managers, and the farm worker is planning to ask for a minimum of £25 a week instead of £16*. Planning

---

* The situation has, of course, improved for the teacher (basic minimum £2,565), but not for the farm labourer (basic minimum £2,028), jumps of just under 150% while the cost of living has jumped 125% approximately from 1971 to 1977.

to – they don't have it yet. What could Captain, Brother, Ambassador, Wesker do with £25 a week? And none of us was super rich, perhaps not rich at all, just comfortable, which meant that we all needed to keep an eye on our bank balances; budgeting was not an alien problem to us. What *are* they discussing? Why don't they simply say that, based on their own experiences of how expensive everything is, average wages are not enough? Why aren't they incredulous at the government's fights to keep wages down, outraged by that on which a worker is expected to be human and happy?

In that moment of pause – and it is ever so brief – it seems to me that they all see it: the big gulf between the haves and the have-nots, the vision of an impending sharpening of the conflict between 'them and us'; and they remember that all industrial disputes are more than an argument about whether the kitty can be raided for a few pence more or not; they are arguments about the inherent injustices of a competitive, free-for-all system, and a real leader on the railwaymen's demands raises questions of morality and not problems of simple mathematics. They see it, pause, reflect, and – it seems to me – feel impelled to move on.

When Business Man comes in he at once declares his support of the government. 'What *I* don't like, and get angry with, are the stories going out, especially our own stories, that the amount offered is miniscule. But *is* it? I mean, *I* don't think the government can afford to pay what the unions demand. But, foolishly, they had their ballot, and we encouraged the ballot –'

'*I* was for the ballot,' the Captain interrupts. 'And I was for the ballot because we all didn't think the men were behind the strike. But we were wrong.' Captain's confession that he and the *Sunday Times* were behind the ballot because they thought the men were not behind strike action staggers me. Even I could have told them that. Being at the centre of a news machine is

H

obviously no guarantee for correct political evaluations. The Captain, I guess, would be the first to admit that; not even being Marx is a guarantee! But that doesn't seem to be the problem; the problem seems to provoke the question: does being a desk journalist, who is trying to make sense of one problem in the brief time left to him before going on to make sense of another problem, guarantee that you'll *never* make the correct political evaluation?

'What *are* the alternatives?' the Captain chairmanises.

'One: bugger all! Two: get the D.P. to provide a second Jarrot review. Three: give in and give them their 14% or 16% or whatever it is. I mean we could write a leader that the country just has to put up with the work to rule, or higher fares, or that the entire railways' financing and accounts system needs reorganising – which is, incidentally, what *I* really believe to be the answer.'

They discuss the miners' break through the wage ceiling. Were they a special case? They all think, yes. Not even they are free from the nation's collective fears of claustrophobia. Our guilts about miners are keenly woven into our childhood myths: miners actually work in those interminable, deep and dungeoned corridors that inhabit ordinary men's nightmares. Give them the money! They might be buried alive under the earth. But railwaymen? They're paid to take joyrides *over* God's earth.

'Right!' says the Captain, 'let's have a show of hands. You're in favour of Marsh paying up?'

'Yes,' says the Ambassador. 'If I'm pushed to the wall, yes, I am. I mean if he doesn't pay up he'll lose so much in fares ... '

'Well, *I* don't believe the government can afford another cave-in,' says the Business Man.

'Oh, no!' says the Ambassador, 'Oh, I think British Transport should pay but not at the price of the exchequer, no! Only at the price of the commuter.'

'And what,' asks Business Man, 'if the CBI grit their teeth and say we'll stick to a 5% rise in prices and Marsh has to raise fares *above* 5% to pay for the pay increase?'

'But is it a 5% rise?' the Ambassador asks. 'Is that what's needed to cover the wage claim? Does anybody know?'

'I must look into that,' says the Captain, and continues: 'Is my idea of Jarrot phase-two ridiculous?'

'Trouble is,' says the Business Man, 'the bulk of all such reports becomes a gloss for the government's failures, and the unions throw all the pages into the wastepaper basket except the ones referring to their increased wages.'

They all consider that perhaps what's needed is simply a guide to the plans – everyone's so confused. No flowery pontifications, just a recapitulation of the possibilities; who's suggesting what: who's saying no; and why.

The Ambassador reminds the Captain that he, the Captain, has the casting vote. 'Brother and I are doves, the Business Man here is a hawk, what are you?'

'I'm beginning to feel a bit hawkish on this one,' the Captain replies; 'in fact, I think *I'll* write something on the railways.'

'Oh, that's a real directive if you like,' says the Ambassador.

From which they go on to discuss 'the right of silence', calling in on the Stockholm conference on the way, French intransigence and, finally, deciding to wait till next week to write about the rail dispute. Of the leaders on that Sunday the first points wearily to government hypocrisy over their environment policy, and the second diplomatically spanks President Pompidou's bottom in language faintly reminiscent of astrological forecasts. I can't resist running a *Nova* prediction for Leo together with the last paragraph of the *Sunday Times* second leader for June 11th, 1972.

'If you intend to make statements from the throne criticising the attitude of your family and near relatives because you feel that you have not of late received the courtesy and respect you deserve, avoid such recriminations around the 16th or you will find yourself—anatomically speaking—out on a limb and with your heart in exile. The new moon on the 20th is in conjunction with the planet Neptune, the influence responsible for so much of the confusion and uncertainty prevalent on the domestic front. Obviously this is the wrong time to take decisions of any consequence affecting the situation in your home. When the sun enters the sign of Sagittarius on the 22nd your optimism and confidence should receive a slight boost, but you would do well to practise a more circumspect and tolerant approach in your personal relationships than is your wont. The new, enlarged E.E.C. will have some vital decisions to take, including agreement on a new Atlantic relationship and on improved relations with Eastern Europe, the Commonwealth and Japan. The autumn summit, and the thorough preparations which should precede it, will be an excellent opportunity for a rational and forward-looking discussion of these issues. Instead of indulging in displays of petulance at not having things all their own way, the French will be better employed helping to prepare constructively for the new, interdependent, Europe of the Seventies.'

The News Room

They tell me to be sure and arrive in the News Room on Saturday. That's when it all happens. I've watched the week start slowly and noted the increased pace as the days passed. Saturday will be the climax. The first important idea comes to me concerning the play. It must be set like *The Kitchen*. All departments on stage at once, the story weaving its way from one group to another; action, movement, dialogue to be continuous, beginning slowly and ending with the hectic activity of the moments just before the pages go down. Perhaps, to the rear of the stage, a large screen of the machines, which, as the end approaches, slowly begin to move and spit out the sheets of newsprint with it's attendant noise in the background.

It's more difficult to make sense of the long, cluttered News Room. It's full of new faces behind the desks which through the week had been empty. The phone rings non-stop; a secretary singing 'News Desk' every five minutes punctuates the chatter. A man comes up to me. 'They tell me you're Arnold Wesker. Writing a new play about us. Very pleased to meet you, been an admirer for a long time.' He, like so many others, provides me with useful and unasked for information. He's a Saturday sub and a weekday official spokesman for the Treasury. 'My wife gets the cheque from the Treasury and I come here to earn my beer money.' There are three others. One 'a Renaissance scholar who writes on obscure poetry by obscure Italian monks. Another who's one of the heads of a B.B.C. overseas news programme. Another who lectures on journalism at the Polytechnic.' I sit in a corner, feel a little foolish and exposed, but it's known why I'm here and many are anxious to guide me. 'Reporters send in good information badly written; the sub is used to give the story a perspective the reporter has lost. Problem is: the subs, who're used to badly written stories, often rewrite the good ones also ... inky-fingered maniacs!'

Snatches of conversation build up what's happening.

'Our copy taker is in chaos and Ian is sitting in his hotel waiting to dictate — can you do something about it? ... Why doesn't he do the pop festival and then I can do Wimbledon? ... We're going down to that wedding. It's royalty and the chief feels a little responsible to them or for them or something ... Ring him up, tell him copy is O.K. but ask him what he means by the top of page 7 where it says "the secret transcripts have been released!" What transcripts have

been released, by whom, to whom and about what? ... Right!
Rand on the front page and Pakistan on the newspage. Rand is
surprised Elsberg could leak so much. We'll believe them ... We'll
put Wilson here, abortion over here. Hanratty down there and
that'll leave the upper right space for the photo of Solti ...'

I ask: 'Can anyone tell me why they're giving front page space
to a 50-year-old opera conductor holding his 14-month-old
baby?' The reply is: 'Well, we've got a story about a 14-year-old
hanging, one about a mother urging her daughter to death in
order to save her from the shame of producing a bastard, a story
about the Common Market which we're all agreed is a turn-off
subject by now, so, with a gruesome front page like that you
need a drop of human warmth to make our millions of readers
like the world just a little bit on their Sunday off work. Right?
Next problem.'

I pick up spare sheets and try to read with the new eyes I've
been given these past days, but it's no good. I still can't get
beyond the first paragraphs of most articles. A treacherous
thought brings me down: newspapers are not boring so much
as they induce a sense of futility. After the first sentences I think:
what the hell! The language is predictable, the facts likely to be
inaccurate and contradicted in another newspaper, or if not
inaccurate then specially selected or incomplete, or the situation
will change tomorrow or something else is more important or
there's just too damn much of it anyway. I'm simply reading
what someone has been interested in for the space of a couple of
hours spent interviewing and typing. I'm being agitated by a
week of someone else's enthusiasm, tossed about by ephemeral
curiosities, whipped up by typewriter emotions. 'The essence of
good journalism,' says someone, 'is to remain bored until the
opportune moment.' I feel dangled on the end of strings, manipulated.

But this day has its special excitement. The front page is being newly designed. The left-hand column is to be extra wide to take a new idea, a kind of 'stop-press' selection of late news items. The head printer is in a panic. I'm not sure if I understand the problem but it's to do with the new column being wider than on the continuation over-sheet. Someone gets irritated. 'Tell him the British have just sent a man to the moon but we're ignoring it because it'll upset the layout of the front page.' The front page is drawn out again and again. Messengers stand around waiting to be given bundles of papers: 'Business News, please.' 'Sports desk, please.' 'Foreign.' 'Processing, please.' The paper is slowly built up, the various editors hovering around a main table where the head layout man draws and re-draws the placement of articles with his ruler. Changes reflect the editors' ideas of which issues are more important than others. The headlines of other papers are scanned, their scoops can alter an entire week of planning. It's a creative process.

PART TWO

'They've lived so long in a world of expenses,
first-class hotels and travel and they can't remember
what it's like to live any other life. I've got old aunts
and uncles and friends of parents I still know. Not
them. That's what's fresh about the underground press,
for all its faults. They don't send people from the
outside, in. They're in already. In the prison, in the
dole queue, in the slum house, in the demonstration.

The machines

It's insisted that I visit the noisy deep of the building in time to
watch the printing machines turn out the first edition. It's vast,
thunderous and impressive. There are nine beauties each capable
of turning out 200,000 papers. Installed over a period of about
six years from 1962 they cost approximately £7 million. Before
completion they already looked out of date compared with the
newest equipment. And the management is now confronted with
having to employ about 2,000 throughout when, I'm informed,
the paper could be produced with a third fewer people.

'The printing machinery is Victorian. I mean consider – we
type out our copy, sub-editors knock it into shape, compositors
type it out again on the linotype machine which produces
proofs needing proofing. When the proofing's approved then
the linotype of each page is assembled into a metal frame
called a forme, copy sheets are hand-pressed from this and
proofed again. Then the forme is put into a large mangle
operation where a soft flabby cardboard is subjected to
considerable pressure to produce a mirror image of the sheet
and by this time it's become something called a flong which
another machine flings into a half-cylindrical shape of lead.
Two half-cylinders make one side of a double sheet so they

have to be bolted to the rotary presses into one end of which you feed a large roll of paper. Barrels of ink are drained into the machines and knobs are guarded to ensure the correct flow and pressure and, when all is ready, you press a button which ends you up with a neatly cut and folded *Sunday Times*. All this instead of using photographic or web-offset techniques with computerised methods of cutting and folding. Why don't we switch? Because it reduces manpower and the unions are protecting the livelihoods of their men. To start a newspaper from scratch you used to need £10 million, today you can do it for £100,000. The implications are tremendous; instead of newspapers being only open to a handful of millionaires it's now possible for you and me to start a paper and the operation could be handled by a girl who'd done a typing course instead of men who'd had to serve a five-year apprenticeship. Typists earn £20 a week, printing craftsmen £60. Who can blame the unions? And they have a very strong weapon. I can remember two occasions on which agreements were signed, sealed and delivered but on the Friday night they changed their mind and asked for more, so we had a pistol at our head. You can't *not* put out newspapers. They know, you see, that it's a declining industry. Sooner or later, they say, we're going to get screwed so we'll make all we can as fast as we can which results in the screw being applied sooner.'

Four things strike me: the noise, the vastness of the operation, the men with withered hands, and the dull, slick smartness of the production managers who seem tough, shrewd and idle. Another treacherous thought brings me down: the arguments demanding just return for the workers' labour have gradually, over the years, also become a false argument glorifying that labour and, here's the treachery, the glorification has grown commensurate with our own thanksgiving for not having to do the soul-destroying jobs ourselves. If we are seen to be defending his rights then the working man's complaints of boredom and humiliation at work are diffused. The more we endow his work with intelligence the less guilty we feel for the satisfactions of our own professions. Deafened by the noise of the machine room I understand that the factors to be considered in a wage claim are not only the rising cost of living or the correct figure for the type of product, or the degree of responsibility or apprenticeship involved but a new factor which could be named 'the undesirability factor'. The less attractive the job the more must be paid for engaging him in it. And the more our society confronts a man with the glamours and pleasures of other worlds the more they are going to have to pay the man whose own world they've made appear less attractive to him. Looking at the men in the machine rooms who retain an incredible cheerfulness, humour and natural intelligence, I find myself thinking not 'how admirable and noble' but 'thank God it's them and not me', and I'm relieved to move out of the noise into the comparative peace of a Saturday upstairs.

> 'The journalist is a kind of actor, he makes his
> decisions only under pressure, when "the world"
> is waiting for the story; hence his reluctance to
> *talk* about a story, because if it's aired, it evaporates.'

The Arts Pages

'We keep ourselves to ourselves, here.' As a literary man I should feel at home in this office. I think I am. At any rate I make a greater success of the pretence that I am. Mild resentments that my book of lectures received scant attention from these arbiters of taste crumble when I discover they receive over 9,000 books a year, the rate increasing yearly, of which they manage to review a fifth. 'What chance the new novels?' I ask. They tell me they're aware of the problem of new novels and give them special attention. 'But we make mistakes and regret certain books we've passed up.' I look through the shelves. Crisp, fresh things; books demand to be possessed. What happens to the review copies? 'We pack off batches to reviewers whose field they are, they decide what to review then keep or sell or give them away. Sometimes people stroll through and take books – we have a critic who's a Japophile with a passion for butterflies, flower arrangements and stone gardens. The rest? They get sold and the money goes into the Thomson account.'

Critics clutter in and out to check their copy, pick up new books, confirm theatre or travel arrangements, complain and gossip. Faces are at last attached to names I've seen each week at the top of a review column: Felix Aprahamian, Cyril Connolly, Julian Symons. One critic asks 'Wouldn't it be better if someone else reviewed this book? I find his writing so awful that I'm beginning to feel it's unfair.' Harold Hobson rings in and I whisper: 'Tell him his favourite playwright sends regards,' thinking he'll say something like 'What's Harold Pinter doing in your office?' But he guesses who it is and we chat, completely ignoring the massive attack I'd written on critics some weeks before. What do I expect? That we should snarl, churlishly ignore one another? It's not easy to be rude and courtesy doesn't prevent me from attacking nor, incidentally, protect me from being attacked.* I don't feel the need to be aggressive to prove where I stand. Nevertheless I'm beginning to feel a little like the journalist who once came to interview me for an article he was writing for

---

* Hobson never did acknowledge my article on critics – 'Casual Condemnations' – published in *Theatre Quarterly* (Vol. 1, No. 2, 1971), but bided his time till a new play came up for review a year later – *The Old Ones* – **then** he leapt!

Private Eye on Centre 42 and the Roundhouse. He regretted coming, he said, because the hard edge of his critical faculty was blunted by my 'charm' which, even so, didn't prevent him making fourteen errors of fact in that truth-at-all-costs public school powder keg.

As arts editors they find especial pleasure feeding me information and stories from behind their three desks which, bumper to bumper brings them daily face to face with each other.

'*Everyone, except us, has to be careful of the Irish edition, Catholic sensibilities, certain omissions for them or copies might be impounded … Do you know that the first edition of most Sunday newspapers is read by competitors at six o'clock on the Saturday evening to see if there's a scoop they've missed which they can then get into their later editions? The really big scoops are not put into the early editions at all, Philby in Moscow, for example … It was at a concert of a Beethoven symphony and Carl Orff's* Carmina Burana, *and our music critic overheard one of the members of the orchestra say, in a loud voice, "now that we've buggered up Beethoven we'd better fuck Orff" … He's not rude, just mannerless … Yes, he writes his reviews by hand, sends them in unpunctuated and when we've knocked them into shape he collects them to store and sell to the university of Texas … The better they are the less they mind your criticism of their reviews, it's only the minor critics who go in for tantrums … The rumour is that he puts deliberate mistakes into his columns in order to attract readers' letters which then provide copy for his next week's column; gets annoyed when the subs correct his galleys … He sort of got the money for his soul without actually selling it … He had a passion, though not now that he has children of his own, for the most exotic mammals … We all take notice of colleagues, look for praise from each other, I can still be affected and placed in seventh heaven if the editor passes me and says, "that was a good piece you wrote last week" … *'

I glance at the mail lying around on desks. Every morning the secretary goes through the ritual of opening fifty or so letters deciding who needs to answer which. I ask if all letters are answered. They are, often by hand. Can I see one? I'm told I can read whatever I like. Many make me blush, they read like those early, pompous letters to editors one used to write as an adolescent.

'Whatever your decision it's bound to prove expensive. If you reject it, you will discover soon, as I have already warned you, that you have missed 'the scoop of the century'. If you accept it and publish the articles I shall expect payment at a rate that will enable me to complete my life's work during the next two or three years.'

The replies are patient and courteous. And poems? 'Oh yes, we receive those all right. World disasters bring them in. And Prince Philip's birthday. Says much for the poetic soul of the British public but hardly contributes to British poetry, I feel.'

The traffic of people is continuous. It seems incredible to me that such a packed and carefully constructed newspaper is ever produced. No one seems to work, they only ever appear to be reading newspapers. In the corridor on the way to the lavatory one of the Insight team stops me. They'd all been affected by my week in their office. 'I was over-reacting like hell, trying to be too casual; and every time we lifted the phone you'd reach for a pen and immediately we all felt we were talking gibberish. As for the editorial conferences I hear they were hamming it up all the time. Everyone playing professional journalist.'

The lavatory paper in Thomson House is of the old-fashioned kind: hard, glossy on one side. It tears at one's tender corners and blocks up the pot; though, it's true, soft packs do run the risk of dirtying one's hands!

On the way back from the toilet a columnist stops me and confesses he occasionally puts trivial items in his column to retain contact with that same person concerning whom a future story is looming up. Meanwhile in the office, a book reviewer who is also a novelist and film-script writer comes in to collect his book for the week and check his proofs: 'Is it your idea of a joke, a correction or an improvement to change my words from "to put it mildly" to "to put it wildly"?' They begin to reminisce over past misprints and another is produced sounding like something from Joyce's *Tales of Shem and Shaun*: 'They become incredibly wound up; yet there is method in their madness for the unwinding is ceremonious and without a bitch.'

My presence makes it irresistible for the book reviewer to air dark grievances. He suggests that writing novels is more difficult than writing plays; I leave it to others to argue that one out. Then his real complaint emerges: new plays command greater attention than new novels, a first night is treated as more of an event than publication day. I'm so eager to concede he's right that I forget to remind him he deals in the ballyhoo of films. But, just as I'm really enjoying being out and about and thinking how pleasant it is to exchange ideas with fellow writers, his real complaint blossoms into a personal grudge. 'I mean,' he says, 'one does get a bit tired of hearing about "our Arnold" ... ' Stay at home, Wesker, any hour can be the hour of the assassin.

> 'A journalist is a man who possesses himself of a
> fantasy and lures the truth towards it.'

I ask about relationships with the outside world. Do literary editors have fraught relationships with publishers and writers? Aren't they anxious about the parties and lunches to which they're invited? Haven't they got a nervous twitch, confronted with sweetness from interested persons? Do they ever know when they're liked for their own sakes? What about my presence? No! No! They love having me around, didn't I want a job? Wouldn't I like to review for them? Delighted to have someone from the outside with comments, suggestions, new conversation; and of course they're worried about being manipulated but what can they do? They listen to those whom they trust and respect, decline when their own instincts are strong, pick winners, losers, have regrets, victories, quarrels with themselves and each other. What can ever be satisfactory in such an unsatisfactory world? They discourage sneers in their reviewers and cover as much as they can without too much loss of seriousness. But they have as many pages as the paper's advertising will allow and advertising is sometimes scarce.

I am to hear this again and again. The big debate between whether a newspaper should depend upon advertising or the sale price for its existence. Three months after decimalisation the *Sunday Times* used the change to creep up from 1/3 to 1/7 (8p), a leap of 27%. Some say it should have gone up to 10p at once, others that it should be 12p, a price increase of 100%. 'If we aim for 50% advertising and 50% from the price of the paper, rather than one third to two thirds as it now is, we might lose the low-income readers but then that would boost the confidence of the advertisers in the readership and it would pay off that way.' (Oh? Do we not want nasty, low-income readers for such a serious paper? Is seriousness only for those who can afford it?) Everyone complains they're not given enough space and advertising gets the blame.

The jostling for room is fierce and involves proclaiming the greater importance of one's own piece over one's colleagues'. The most aggressive journalists are the youngest: arrogant and left wing; though the *Sunday Times* still has old-fashioned veins enough to dilute even their hot blood. It's a journal with bits and pieces of socialists floating around like flotsam 'after the havoc caused by their rise into affluence'. However, guilts make them fight harder for their good causes and hustle brusquely for their space. The older and cannier ones have other methods. 'The thing to do is try and get a foothold at the top of the next page and press down. It's more difficult to press up.'

I ask, why not allow critics to review the plays they like and merely mention those they despise, and if that means there's only 100 words in the theatre column one week, so what? The reply is that people opening their Sunday papers look forward to reading a critic's piece and would be disappointed to miss it even though it were an indifferent bumbling on. And as for the critic himself! What? Him give up his precious space?

My next question commands immediate respect; how much does a journalist give himself to his paper? Ah! there you have it. Sooner or later everyone is forced to make the decision between family and newspaper, between public dedication and private responsibility, between wearying battles for power and demeaning squabbles of wedlock. There is the odd reporter who begs to be sent abroad to avoid his wife or family, others develop mild (some not so mild) schizophrenia. 'What I want to do is slide around having little conversations, but I can't quite give up the glamour of catching a plane and having access to important people.' Most simply become tired.

'And one grows old, you've no idea, at 32 one is old already ... You feel it when you've got deputies under you; being people's deputies is an invitation to an assassination; if you do you create a bad atmosphere, so I didn't. But now I've got a deputy under me I have to work out what my attitude is. Do I encourage him, push him? I do, but I wonder. Credit grabbing is one of the sicknesses of the profession, it takes it out of you ... You can tell he plays the power game because he's so bad at it, frustrating really, wasteful ... When Kruschev was sacked, this reporter, one of our top men, tried to *phone through to the Kremlin. Didn't stop to think that neither of them would be able to speak the other's language, just automatically reached for the phone. The spark goes. Last night on TV I was watching the awful tragedy of the three Russian astronauts dying in space and I was thinking — yes, now how can we handle that? This way? Yes, maybe. That way? Yes, well — I'll sleep on it. Years ago I'd have immediately rung up people and started generating ideas ... If you're young and in charge and you want to deflate an older journalist my advice to you is: when he brings his piece you flip through it and then throw in on the desk and say, "Well, honestly, I didn't expect you to show me something like this." ... If you invade people's private lives it swarms over the organisation of your life ... We were out to get him and then he went out to get us, it all grew very ugly and vicious and ended up in a personal vendetta. I wanted to get all I could on the man to hang, knife and destroy him utterly and he attempted to do the same to us, ringing up our wives and telling them to get their husbands to lay off or else ... '*

'That's what a journalist sees as his function: naming
the guilty men — his yardstick is one of unswerving
idealism.'

Another editorial conference

The editor has a knack of ignoring sour remarks and the under-current tensions which betray themselves through the odd, demolishing comment: 'Yes, it's a nice quiet piece.' He employs a candour which sets him among his colleagues rather than a patronising tolerance which would place him outside them. Someone tells me this story about him: 'I was sitting in the editor's office with the editor's two secretaries watching tennis on his TV set when he walks in with a fellow director. He steps back, embarrassed to have intruded. "Sorry," he says, "I'll go somewhere else."' At this conference he wears a maroon shirt and silver tie which reminds me of a 1920s Chicago mobster. The conference begins.

'What's happening on the Dimbleby TV programme? I thought it was very good actually. But then I've changed my mind six times on it already so I'm not a very reliable witness.'

'There's a letter for you in our pigeonhole from a Pakistan official saying how disappointed he is that such a distinguished newspaper could lower itself, etc., etc., and he's cutting his subscription.'

'I think we ought to have a very good reporter in India in case something blows up between her and Pakistan. It's a fascinating situation – no, I mean really, we ought to be there, in case war breaks out.'

Someone raises their hand. 'Me, please. But I think the Naxalite situation is even more important, more than anyone thinks.'

'What about the fishermen of England and the Common Market?'

'You and Peter look into the fishermen, will you? By the way, what about our new news digest on the front page, any comments?'

'I don't quite know what the journalistic theory is.'

'Well, it's a service. It's also a good design breakthrough. Our front page is less old-fashioned now.'

'Our middle pages are still full of old-fashioned layout, though.'

'Yes, and I think we ought to take a look at those too, get them to look more like the magazine.'

'Problem is, our layout is still dictated by old advertising agency agreements which keep us stuck to the old column widths.'

'That article on convenience foods, is it a big story or not?'

'I thought we were going to find out *if* they are being sold bullshit.'

'If they're not being sold bullshit, it's not a good story.'

'I'm very bored with the issue of shelling peas.'

So, the situation in India is 'fascinating', is it. War might break out! What else do I expect? That they should maintain a sombre or thunderous manner at all times? I train myself to catch the inverted commas they place around their statements. Everyone is terrified of making a fool of himself. No opinion or suggestion can be proffered too sonorously. Sentiment and passion must be reserved for the story itself. Among themselves they must appear controlled, aloof, disengaged. I subdue offended sensibilities and try to be 'mature' about it. If war breaks out there *should* be a good reporter there. The *prevention* of the war is something to be attended to elsewhere, by other means. The doctor doesn't weep while contemplating what the diagnosis is, nor even when he plunges in the scalpel that may heal.

> 'People sitting around in offices, lost, that's all a
> newspaper is, sitting around waiting for ideas to
> come, wondering what the hell to do next.'

Look!

Look!'s office contains wasted women. 'It isn't the most scintillating week's work, is it? All that effort and we have a column dealing with birds, male sterilisation and the men who make suits for £130 each.' Women are always more impressive than men; they seem to intuit truths and real motivation. Much more compelling than the dreary brilliance of men who are simply 'well informed'. 'We should be provocative as well as practical. "Down with children", "must mothers of handicapped children be martyrs?"—that sort of thing ... and we should be more visual, forced to look for the more potent image than the brilliant phrase. I love being stretched. After all, we earn a good wage and I feel I ought to deserve it ... '

A young man brings in a canvas chair; simple, wooden deal struts, screwed into shape, the canvas glued and tacked. It's low slung, unvarnished and cheap. He's asked to leave it with them for a few days. If they decide it's good value for money they'll promote its virtues, saying where it can be bought and for how much; but nothing will indicate it's an advert and a percentage of the sales will go to the *Sunday Times*. The information surprises me. Don't I remember that if a group of M.P.s take space to argue an issue they must pay for it and the print will be boxed in saying, 'This is an advertisement' to prevent it being confused with editorial copy?

A letter from a reader creates interest and the promise of a story. She writes saying she knows a family—'a lovely little family'—with two children, where the husband was refused a sterilisation operation on the National Health and had to pay £30 to get it done privately. Hands are rubbed, it seems their other article on male sterilisation has started something, miniature battle stations are called; they'll do something more about this one in view of the problems of population explosion. Look! is very concerned about too many people in the world eating up resources. But, coincidentally, I happen to glance through their book of back numbers and find that, on August 30th, 1970, there was an article on the negligees created by a beautiful black designer, Rose Lewis of Knightsbridge, who herself was seductively modelling one of her creations. She is quoted, with that obvious delight the English take in their unserious, unpretentious light-hearted view of this sad, old world, as saying: 'I'm proud to have played my part in the population explosion and I feel responsible for early wedded bliss in many marriages.'

'I feel that our role is to slightly balance the serious, if not ponderous, side of the paper by articles which are, yes, slightly titillating.' 'Sexually titillating?' I ask. 'Yes.' It worries me that they use the word titillating and I press them again: is that what they really mean? 'After all,' I say, 'the word means "cheap thrills".' They retract; no, that's not what they mean. Such loose use of words desperately trying to make the world seem a gayer place appears to produce a philosophy of light-heartedness which is not only sloppy but sometimes dishonest. As a result of a series about a fat girl getting into attractive clothes, and feeling not exactly happy but at least unanguished about her size, many letters came in asking how she did it. The letters caused some embarrassment because on investigation it was found that some of the photographs didn't show her back where gaping holes betrayed that the dresses could not be done up. This story is not relished either as a boast or a confession but emphasises the sense they feel of trivial pursuits. 'We're supposed to be good at gossip and writing about boys and knickers. You have to be Mary McCarthy or mistress of an editor to be sent to Vietnam. Even Mary McCarthy had to pay for herself.' Neither is their pretence of 'unseriousness' always echoed in their columns. Tucked between the 'knickers and boys' stories are occasional anonymous pieces, like the articles by a woman about her depressed husband, a stark and moving account reflecting the heart of many relation-ships, worthy of the opening paragraphs of a good novel.

As with every group I encounter they arm me with anecdotes.

'Seventeen of us from the Sunday Times *once wrote different chapters of a book called* I Knew Daisy Smutten? *and the publisher held a party for us at his house. Thought us very low indeed he did. And when, after a power cut which brought complete darkness to the party, the lights came back on again, he was caught clutching two priceless pieces of sculpture to his chest ... And so Shelley Winters*

*says to this reporter, "Vittorio Gassman and I were just mad about
each other physically and couldn't keep our hands off each other if we
were in the same room. Then he learned to speak English and I
learned Italian and we found we hadn't a thing in common" ... We
have a very strange house nurse on the* Sunday Times. *One girl
went up to her and asked for something stronger than aspirin as she'd
had a series of continuous headaches. "Oh," said the nurse, "you've
probably got a tumour on the brain!" ...What do we do with all
these books we receive? Oh, wait till they accumulate, then sell them
and occasionally indulge in rounds of champagne ... a prawn
omelette was his idea of an exotic night out ... Can't move a cabinet
or a chair or even change a plug on your own; must call the men
from downstairs or there'd be a strike ... '*

Printing error in Look! February 28th, 1971: Headline: 'Controlling Sex — by Lord Fisher. This is an extract from the former
Archbishop of Canterbury's new book, *Control of Sex*, to be
published on Friday at £1·75 ... '

Apology in the following week's edition: 'Lord Fisher's book
from which Look! extracted a chapter last week is called *Touching
on Christian Faith* and will be published ... '

Look! blames the agent.

One issue produces an interview with a famous playwright
and his wife about their clothes. It seems out of character and I
ask how the interview was conducted. Was it a wide-ranging
discussion over many subjects out of which the interviewer
extracted choice quotes? Someone tells me, 'no', the couple were
told it would only be about their clothes and that that was how
they actually spoke. Did I think it made them look ridiculous?
Hoping it doesn't sound offensive, I say 'yes'. Then comes the
shock: so did they.

'But don't you feel they ought to have been warned?' I ask.

'No, they've been in the game a long time, they know what

words appear like in print. The piece wasn't a distortion.'

'Not a distortion of those one and a half hours,' I say, 'but those one and a half hours may distort the whole picture of their lives.'

'Oh, I don't know, it's only a portion.'

'But do you believe every portion, every wart needs to be magnified? Is that the price to be paid for being allowed to be a writer?'

'People in public life know what they're exposed to.' Someone observes that I'm asking serious questions about a flip piece and I feel foolish at disturbing a kind of cult of frivolity. Poor artist! While attempting to be a 'man of the world', thinking that's the way the world is: publicity at any price, he's lured into making such a fool of himself.

One lunch-time there's an 'ideas conference'. French bread, cheese, a bottle of red wine and a thick strawberry and cream laden cake baked by my wife for the occasion. They toy with the idea of a series on people's obsessions; another on 'my best friend'. Who should start it? I suggest Bernard Levin. The unseriousness of the English coupled with the 'inverted comma' tone of newspaper chat is very intimidating but I risk offering them an idea for a series: 'the morality of fashion'. I quote them Ruskin: 'But whatever happens to you, this, at least, is certain, that the whole of your life will have been spent in corrupting public taste and encouraging public extravagance. Every preference you have won by gaudiness must have been based on the purchaser's vanity; every demand you have created by novelty has fostered in the consumer a habit of discontent; and when you retire into inactive life, you may, as a subject of consolation for your declining years, reflect that precisely according to the extent of your past operations, your life has been successful in retarding the arts, tarnishing the virtues, and confusing the manners of your country!' I must have been mad.

PART THREE

'I'm in it to get rid of all my phobias and hang-ups,
to have a go at *them*. It's all entertainment, isn't it?
You can't underestimate the man in the street, he
makes up his own mind, doesn't he? Doesn't
believe any of it. And I'm aiming at all those
middle-class fascists anyway. It's all a joke. They
love it. Feel honoured to be attacked.'

Bi-annual pep talk

A hundred people sit in the director's dining room trying to
appear at ease. Not everything I hear can be repeated, but some?
Surely! I can't resist it.

'No big declarations. Circulation gone up fantastically, even
with the price rise, and it's the biggest rise in the history of this
paper and certainly in Fleet Street ... what a terrific success story
that is ... and with the Sunday newspaper market contracting ...
our problem is that like everyone else we're dependent on the
British economy. Recession, slump? Then no advertising ... but
don't get depressed ... we're editorially very strong. I'm grateful
for all the scoops. I don't know how we do it week after week.
Personally I think we could have got away with a price rise of
10p, let alone 8p. I believe in a high-priced newspaper, we can't
depend on advertising for ever ... Some things have been
helpful ... If you take everything in the last budget: corporation
tax, S.E.T., profits tax, the lot, it all used to be no good to the
company. Such improvements don't, of course, alter our
editorial policy towards the government ... '

Someone asks, referring to some figures mentioned, 'What do
they mean in percentages?'

Answer: 'I don't think I've worked out percentages. You've
got to give me notice of a question like that.'

Questioner: 'I didn't have notice of your speech.'

Everyone pretends not to take the gathering's purpose seriously, but a childlike delight is in their eyes to be told they've done so well. They feel sheepish these grown, powerful, opinion-making men and woman, sitting together, being reminded of school days again. And suddenly it occurs to me, as I look at them, that the attractive quality of the journalist is the aura of other people's power which he carries around with him. He functions in excitements other people create. Now, as I watch them, huddled together and stripped of their individual columns, made one – and vulnerable – by their common attentiveness to the dear Captain's words, I can see it. And that pirated aura gives their opinions an intimidating but borrowed aggressiveness while relieving them of action and the responsibility of action; the existence of Captains always speaks of relieved responsi-bilities.

> 'They play this great game at work and then they
> shuffle home on the commuter train to suburbia.
> They need this fantasy world to compensate for
> their lives.'

Half-time

My third week comes to an end and I feel it's time to try and organise some preliminary thoughts. Is there a journalistic mind? Does it only come alive with the smell of blood? Is contact with men and women who are giants in their field a sad and inevitable enticement to lilliputian attitudes? 'The demeaning sneers of routine journalistic accounts' is a phrase Nick Tomalin uses in the book on Crowhurst. But journalism involves more than routine accounts. I'm told journalists become cross when academics refer to their work as 'instant history'. On the other hand someone confessed he was terrified by notions of 'considered and responsible journalism'. Facts need to be known but because it's recognised that fact is not truth, therefore interpretation is attempted. Opinions are offered. The function is valid but what factors prevent the honest performance of the function? Has anyone named them? Have guards been erected against them? Literature can touch truth because the writer measures and relates facts to his own imperfections in order to arrive at understanding. Few journalists dare measure what they write alongside their own private behaviour, hence so much maudlin sympathy, no real pity, and all idealism is suspected of being pretentious. 'The real resentment against "do-gooders' is that they're so impractical. So you try to shoot them down and then you realise you're a big wolf with a stick knocking at a fly and then you get a conscience and feel you want to help them.' There's confusion and often tortured self-searching. 'There's the archangel and the cynic in all of us; the archangel embarrasses and produces the cynic.' The flow between offices is significant. It's a movement of people sniffing each other out, cuddling up for warmth and reassurance. Ideas are tested on colleagues. Producing a newspaper finally necessitates, despite the quarrels, working together in a close co-operation which produces a bonhomie, loyalties, a sense of purpose and even — yes, though they might shudder — brotherhood; and this creates the illusion that something 'brotherly' is being done. Accuse the journalist of being a snide, hunting, destructive animal and he will flinch, be hurt and surprised, because he can only remember the excitement of having worked together with brilliant colleagues and chummy good-old-working-class-printing-men. He can only recall the infectious enthusiasm of sharing 'hot history', the satisfying weariness of staying up late to get the story right, the friendships that remain after the battles over space and story priorities. All that sweet, shared endeavour leads them to forget that what the endeavour produces may not itself be sweet.

Contempt is difficult for them to conceal. They've met everybody, talked with all sorts, and are themselves terrified of being quoted on anything.

> 'The thing is they aren't giving out prepared speeches so they can't remember what they said, in this way you can always improve on what they said and make it appear as if they've spoken in good English ... One of the lessons of the Maxwell case is that you should never go overboard in praise of any business man, always play it safe and leave openings for yourself ... My contempt for the Western European business man is increasingly extending to the whole spectrum of human beings ... There is no trade unionist who I cannot buy with an overload of food or drink or money, my expenses are the highest in Thomson House because it costs so much to bribe trade union officials ... I find most people so boring in what they say that my slow longhand is fast enough to catch what's worthwhile ... Weinstock is one of the most intelligent men we've met who is more intelligent than us, and we don't meet many of them ... '

Perhaps it's for this reason that, though he cares, the journalist only feels comfortable (or safe?) in the destructive tone of voice. You rarely find a journalist celebrating, except in the Business News where certain makers of money impress by their forceful handling of men or the rise of their profits dividend. It wouldn't occur to them to admire the civilised failure, not in print anyway —but more of them later. Nor is the sad, but heartily brave, tone of self-contempt missing either.

> 'I believe in the capitalist system so I have no conflicts. Conflicts? Hah! I've been looking for them for years; always wanted to be able to resign on a matter of principle ... Professional standards? I don't believe journalists have a profession, I don't know what that pro-

fession is anyway, and certainly they don't have standards. It's the law of the jungle and not a very colourful one ... No one should take any notice of attacks from Private Eye. The best people don't. I mean most people are proud to be there. You only find journalists suing, they're the first to reach for their solicitor ... It's like being in a pub and as long as your wallet is full any number can play and you know at the end of the day no one can question your motives, you can't be done for it. As little as you have the right to do it so no one has the right to judge or stop you ... And when there's a drive to cut expenses in all departments everyone makes their moral pitch to defend their fraudulent demands ... Then after a while one gets sick of hotels and the quick friendships with people about whom one has finally to write something unsympathetic ... I mean, if you go to Ulster and look at the journalists there, sitting around in pubs, drunk, and a bomb goes off in the Falls Road so they draw lots who should go and bring the story back for all of them; it's screwy. Tell you what, the best reporter in Ulster is the barman. He tells them there's an explosion and they all rush to their phones. And these are the men upon whom the world relies for its information.'

'When I'm in a tight corner, worried about a hole in my space, I know there's a pile of *Wall Street Journals* sitting there and I can always rely on them to provide me with a story — that and the *Essex Recorder*. Of course that's how all overseas journalists work, they read the local newspapers and send back precis reports.'

Business News

When I ask, can I sit around in their large office for a week or so, I'm told of course, I'm welcome. Why, they were even beginning 'to feel neglected and feared you'd bypass us. We were told "Wesker won't visit you, you're the heart of the capitalist society he despises".' Can journalists really operate only with such simplified images? Someone has assured me in a previous week: 'The greatest thing about Business News is that they tend to deal with finance as theatre.' And sure enough, on my first day, I'm greeted by a strikingly dramatic and breathless voice (whose breathlessness is due to the fact that it's sardonically laughing at what it's saying at the same time as it's saying it): 'We've been told, ha ha, by the *Telegraph*, ha, ha, ha, that we're like the, ha, TV power game programmes, ha ha ha, tending to see all business as a jungle and all business men as nasty, ha, wrangling, ha, sly, ha, grinning, ha, smooth handshaking, ha, and back-stabbing villains ... ' I become anxious as to whether he'll make it to the end of the sentence. He does. The anxiety is worth it. Far from them being pillars of capitalist society they seem to me an army of very bright urban saboteurs. 'You see, it's a question of the credibility of the *Sunday Times* which, as an old conserva-tive family newspaper, commands more respect than, say the *Observer*, which is known for its liberal policies, and therefore we're a better journal through which to infiltrate radical views — more people will believe us.' The sardonic spirit pervades each one of them.

Or, almost each one. 'I believe Arnold Weinstock was success-ful because he started at the top.' This promises to be interesting — Mr Weinstock* is about to become the personality of my week with them. 'The great thing about him is he's so sane. "The man's no good?" he asks. "Can he go now? Before five o'clock? Why wait?" And indeed, why wait?' I deem it wise not to answer. Good journalists must record. 'If he has to sack 5,000 men because of waste he'll do it. Why not? And he'll justify it by say-

---

* Now Lord Weinstock.

ing it's better for the sacked one because men get depressed
hanging around doing nothing, they lose their self-respect.' Ah
yes, I say to myself, that'll catch in your throat, men losing their
self-respect for not being given machines to mind. Compassionate man, Weinstock. 'And those that stay know that
they're good because Weinstock has kept them and so they're
men of confidence, they work harder.' A Solomon, no less.
But I'm foolish and ponder 'Solomon's' motives. Greed? My
earnest companion disabuses me. 'Waste! Waste offends him,
makes no sense. It's only incidentally that his policy produces
more profits – and don't raise a wry eyebrow at that.' I try not
to raise a wry eyebrow at that. It's easy; everyone is so friendly
and honest.

In fact, as I write this piece, I make the discovery of what it
must sometimes *feel* like to be a journalist – a shit! There's no
problem at all in forgetting the human part I've enjoyed and
exploited while plotting and writing the 'objective' appraisal.
An important lesson, this – not a task I'll undertake many times.

News reaches me that a chapel meeting is due to take place to
discuss the engagement of a currently celebrated women's
lib writer on to the paper. (Apparently there's a separate N.U.J.
chapel for the *Sunday Times* alone, instead of a chapel for all the
Thomson newspapers throughout the country. 'It's the ship
deserting the sinking rat!') The general opinion is that management has over-reached itself and tried to get her in through the
back door. 'I know all about this because I got in on a fiddle
myself though you mustn't believe everything I say. They told
me you need three years' minimum experience in the provinces;
but there are exceptions to that if you're a specialist writer and I
got hired as a specialist in industrial law – industrial relations,
that is, with special reference to industrial law. Of course the
union said, "Ho ho! no such thing. We've heard of industrial
relations but what law?" "Ho ho!" says I, "have you ever had an

industrial relations bill before? Still not convinced? All right," I
says, "I may be wrong but let me work for six months on the
Sunday Times and then you can decide." So, I wrote stuff no one
could understand, conducted seminars up and down the country
and then, finally, pleaded my case on the basis that, though it's
outrageous that I'm here—I'm here! And from that moment on
I was determined to see that no one like me ever got in again so
at once I became a union leader.'

I guess that the wit is for my benefit but it's one of those
doubletake revelations: 'I want to tell you this but don't take
any notice of me telling you.' Still, it doesn't hide the genuine
conflict between a real problem of unemployment in the profession where journalists want to maintain openings for their
colleagues, and their generous desire not to smother talent. Both
sides play around with each other and manoeuvre to save face.
In the final confrontation the shrewd, calm N.U.J. official says
to management, 'Well, we can't black her copy, we don't want a
strike, but if you push me against the wall I'll have to do it. So,
what's to be the compromise?' 'At which point,' staff reports of
management, 'the management jumps up in great relief and
offers, grateful to be let off the hook, one: no one new to be
employed for a year; two: no sackings; three: no dismissals
without consultations with the unions.' It sounds as though
management have given away nothing and we can eagerly
await her first assault.

> 'It's not a pleasant spectacle seeing journalists in a
> bar boast of how they've revealed to the world the
> way in which they saw seventeen people die that
> day at the hands of fascist beasts.'

Business News covers a large area of the fourth floor, a news
paper on its own which alone brings in £3 million a year from

I

advertising.* They can't be wholly subversive about the hands which feed them and though they like to present a Bolshie image to the world they're not really open to the suggestion of an alternative to a capitalist system. The establishment need have little fear of the brilliant left-wingers lurking behind the columns of news and views, it will take more than the *Sunday Times* to crack the ramifications of this country's deeply entrenched and widely accepted competitive spirit. 'One is more likely to fumble towards a desirable state through a competitive society than an autocratic one.' I'm not sure I understand why these are the only two alternatives to consider, but journalists do enjoy talking with each other even though they frequently don't listen to each other. Their stream of words is exuberant and endless—full of opinions about everything, everyone, everywhere, as though the world were full of ghosts asking questions.

'The civil service is capable of responding to orders but they argue too brilliantly with ministers who are not sufficiently clear on their own ideas ... The lawyer by definition is a nihilist because if he's great, he says, "my job is to defend people to the law not the law to people" ... But much more important than the shareholders was that the public was swindled, shareholders deserve what they get, trying to make money work for them instead of working for themselves ... People who fuck up the system appeal to me ... He's 65, lives in Switzerland and is the only man I know who can reach into his back pocket and produce enough cash to buy a company. Made his money out of a cheap record-changing device, £20 million, and has just emerged from opulent retirement to make a bid for B.S.A. Started off by imagining he could make his fortune out of surgical machinery but did what few others did, which is: he actually took the trouble to get himself qualified as a surgeon in order to test whether his inventions

* This figure will obviously have increased since 1971.

worked. Very strange man, hates unions. He's an elitist fascist but
not wholly without charm ... I agree! £400 million paid back to
the international banks leaving £500 millions to pay means nothing
to the man in the street. Who can comprehend that? They only know
that the rich get richer and the poor get poorer. But, today, poverty
is your own fault, today you can stand on your own two feet, anyone
can become Prime Minister. Our beloved leader has proved it, the
nasty Chancellor has proved it; all of them self-made and nasty men
saying you too can also all be self-made and nasty men ... '

A telephone rings: 'There's a lunatic negotiator for the T.G.W.U.
up in the Midlands who, because he's so bored with the usual
demands of his head office, believes that every new contract he
draws up on behalf of his workers has got to have at least one
original clause in it. This time he's insisted that every man get a
day off on his birthday. Anybody interested?' It is difficult to
trace the pattern of what's happening. As with every other
department it seems that all they do is read newspapers. 'Even
on the fourth day,' I'm assured, 'you will think that the paper
can't possibly appear.' But empty desks hint at journalists out on
a job, and the fact that pulls of copy keep coming up from 'the
stone' suggests someone has done some writing somewhere at
some time. Even so, how is it all covered? As I linger on they
build for me a picture of the vast industrial and economic net-
work. Industry: sub-divided into heavy, light, state-owned and
private. Economic management. Industrial relations. International
monetary control. The stock market. Take-overs and the
interpretation of balance sheets. The impact of new technology.
And most of those headings are multiplied, and hence complicated, when dealt with on an international scale. Can they be
handled responsibly by such a small staff even though most are
first-class honours graduates? (One journalist is pointed out as
having a double first in classics, 'went straight to the *Financial*

Times'.) There can be no complaint that they know nothing about industry from the inside, many come from industry and at least one left a number two job on Business News to spend two years in industry, which he gave up in disgust to return to the paper in a less senior position.

I catch myself enjoying their company. It's partly that sardonic tone with the double edges which repel and compel at the same time, but it's also because these weeks in the *Sunday Times* offices remind me of the pleasures of working with people instead of the terrifying, paranoia-making isolation of working alone at home. ('There's a plot afoot to rehabilitate Arnold Wesker,' writes one journalist in the *Guardian*, throwing me into a new fit of paranoia as I sit at home working on this piece. He's reviewing the simultaneous appearance of my book of short stories, and a good, critical study of my plays.

> 'The elegant sneer is admired and if it's like Pope
> it's very good indeed. Problem is it's rarely like Pope.'

Weinstock is the glamour boy of the moment and I hear him discussed endlessly. It's obviously imperative to read the profile on him to discover what there is about shopkeepers that excites and mesmerises the intelligent journalists of Business News. 'When Weinstock came into G.E.C. via an 8·5 million takeover of his father-in-law's firm, Radio and Allied, his prime task was to weed out waste.' A gardener! 'There was waste in design ... There was £10 million (at a time when G.E.C. had £20 million overdraft) tied up in 32 now scrapped regional headquarters!' So? Weinstock tidied it up, big deal! Is big business so badly run that when a man comes along and does, for a great deal of money, simply what he's supposed to do, he's called a genius? A quartermaster, that's all! Finally, when all is said and done, he'll contribute nothing more to our understanding of pain or other men, he'll add nothing beautiful to the world. He's not even an inventor, just a tidy-upper who can resist the need to be loved; an efficient, money-making man, but hard, who has no qualms about sacking and ordering men around; which is not his fault, he'll say, because the world demands efficiency, men depend upon it, someone must pay the price. Very convenient.

But it can't be anything so simple that commands the respect of Business News journalists. Perhaps it is that though Weinstock appeals to men's sense of greed and he must, paradoxically, elicit from them a high degree of co-operation in order to satisfy that greed. The men under him must work unselfishly for their privileges. 'This continuous dialogue between Stanhope Gate (Weinstock's headquarters) and the companies is dedicated to uncovering the truth in each situation. Business men like running away from unpleasant facts. But Weinstock's approach,' writes our good business journalist, 'is exactly that of a good business journalist, determined to cut through half truths and vague generalisations. One of his great strengths is that he never believes anything, and himself says, "All information is suspect".' It is left to the sardonic voice of another good business journalist to cap the Weinstock image. 'Arnold Weinstock's attitude is rather like that of the baron of whom it was asked: why do you build your walls so high and strong? To which he replied: in order to give the peasants' hovels something to lean upon.'

Yet alongside the journalist eulogising Weinstock's iron hand is the journalist rushing to defend the humanity of the *Sunday Times* management. 'As for how ruthless we are, huh! Do you know we had a woman on the travel page who regularly, for two years, used to write a piece saying such and such a place was a lovely sunny beach until the Jews got there! Two years! We never printed it of course but it took us two years before she was sacked. And the ——'s editor! Terrible man! But it took us seven years to pluck up the courage to retire him at 53 on a pension plus a paying consultancy job for five years. Yet there are nice, liberal men on the *Observer* who are beastly to each other, awful!'

My favourite story about Business News is of the time everyone was trying to find a name for the business gossip column. At last someone came up with the name of Prufrock which, most seemed to recall, was the name of a tough, respectable business man in an Eliot poem. Twenty-four hours before going to press the editor asked, 'Why and who, Prufrock?' And the poem was proudly brought out:

No! I am not Prince Hamlet, nor was meant to be;
Am an attendant lord, one that will do
To swell a progress, start a scene or two,
Advise the prince; no doubt, an easy tool,
Deferential, glad to be of use,
Politic, cautious, and meticulous;
Full of high sentence, but a bit obtuse;
At times, indeed, almost ridiculous —
Almost, at times, the fool.
I grow old ... I grow old ...
I shall wear the bottoms of my trousers rolled.
Shall I part my hair behind? Do I dare to eat a peach?
I shall wear white flannel trousers, and walk upon the beach.
I have heard the mermaids singing each to each.
I do not think that they will sing to me.

After the silence there followed agonising hours while everyone stamped around through other books and poems and Roget's *Thesaurus* trying to find a new name until, weary, they decided, inappropriate or not, Prufrock, damn it, was a good name.

'Fink is an abusive term for someone upon whom the journalist relies for his information. The name reveals our love-hate relationship with our job.'

Someone from Insight comes down to Business News and reports: 'I've just had an earbending fink on the telephone who says he's got damaging documents which will implicate Mr A.' 'Oh,' says a sweet-looking, baby-faced but bearded financial tipster, 'are we rubbishing Mr A? He's a con man but we all love him; he's the most charming con man in the food industry, if that's what you can call it.' They say they'll see the fink and I ask whether I can be in at the meeting. They say, with pleasure! if the fink doesn't mind. The next day he arrives with a friend. I remind the journalists that I want to attend and they ask the fink. My guess is that he doesn't quite hear what their request is and imagines I'm simply another journalist – he says yes.

The fink's story

He says, with that jocular English modesty (which, with zany irrelevance, makes me think the English could never be avant-garde about anything because they're too hearty), he says: 'I'm a plumber,' when what he means is he's an engineer. The basis of his story, which I listen to with incredulity, my eyes growing wider and wider each moment much to the amusement, I suspect, of the two journalists, is this: he had discovered, after minute research, that Mr A's stated share price since 1967 was based on a false market and that Mr A was able to achieve this through a complicated system of interlocking holdings which worked roughly in this way; the English company takes over a French company which is then able to buy shares in the subsidiary of the English company which then buys ... and so on. The *Sunday Times* journalists sit patiently and listen. They do so for three hours, committing themselves to little more than an observation about A being 'our favourite crook' while concentrating mostly on pertinent questions that will draw out the fink's motives. He seems to have done a fantastic amount of research and from his briefcase produces balance sheets as published in the *Financial Times* and graphs he's drawn based on those balance sheets. 'And there's this woman in high French financial circles who's also managing director of his French company — running with the hare and hunting with the hounds — so it's all open and conforms absolutely with the letter and spirit of French law, which isn't saying much, and it all looks lovely, a respected housekeeper at the top, very attractive.'

I begin to feel pleased with myself that I can understand so much about high finance and then he utters his first give-away. 'Of course I bought his shares at 71 and sold them at 93 on the basis of what I knew he was going to do. I'd been following him so closely that I understood his pattern of behaviour, his psychology as it were.' Well, I think, *that's* not nice, Mr Fink. At half-time I break to ask if they want any drink, coffee or something. They say they would like anything liquid. The secretaries are reluctant to supply me, offering excuses like 'no clean cups, no water in the kettles, no milk.' I return, defeated and apologetic, but it's not my house. Ten minutes later, however, a secretary appears with a tray of coffee. 'I was overcome with remorse,' she says.

He continued producing his crowded sheets of figures and graphs and talks with a growing agitation that's sexual, as though he's making love to his theme. Elegant arm, hand and finger gestures describe in the air the patterns of his research. The journalists stop him to suggest here and there flaws in his case, which he concedes but balances with more and more evidence. 'The mafia in all this is snuff,' he says. 'Oh, don't laugh, don't laugh.' He reaches into his briefcase for cuttings from German magazines. 'Snuff is the new narcotic, you can put your L.S.D. in it and the kids in Germany and Sweden are all taking it up.' Where is it all leading? His saga seems many-vaulted and endless.

Then, for no apparent reason he tells the story of a well-known banker giving money to two old people in order to help them set up a chocolate factory. A straightforward account except that he refers to the old people as being 'two Jews from Vienna'. I tell myself to sit still and not be so sensitive. But I notice the *Sunday Times* men refer, with too deliberate care I feel, not to the 'Jews from Vienna' but to 'those Viennese immigrants'. Then he says how a friend of his sees Mr A constantly in the company of Mr B and C – both well-known Jewish financiers. Then he talks about another character in his saga as 'an old German Jew'. At which point they try to get him away from such asides and ask: 'It must be very frustrating never having met the man?'

'Good lor, no!' he replies. 'I don't ever want to meet him. I'm so dead against him that I'm frightened of being seduced by his charm. It's much better this way. I've read a file on him *this* thick, and I've followed his manoeuvring this way and that, watched how he's approached first this one for capital, then moved to that one, then tried another attack and realised there's nothing to be gained and so moved on. I've watched him wheedling back and forth and studied his mentality, looked at his handwriting, lived with his thinking for six months – oh no! I know him much better this way. I know him *intimately*.'

His excitement reaches a climax, he's been listened to so well and attentively, been so praised for his research that his guard lowers and, his eyes agitated by a sinister intelligence, he confesses his passion: 'I'm obsessed by the European Jewish Mafia and I've been reading about them going as far back to the time when Napoleon freed the Jews. I mean, think about it, there's the tightly knit X's family together with Y and Z on the Continent, and Messrs. A, B and C on this side of the Channel, and with the Common Market round the corner ... ' He brings his two hands together, locking elegant curled fingers into elegant curled

fingers. ' ... click! The opportunity they've been waiting for —
a highly closed plot in the traditional Jewish manner. But I'm
not,' he adds, 'at all anti-semitic. Only you must see that they're
trying to dominate the new and most important areas of leisure
and food.'

I can't stay to hear more. The description of the plot has already
made me late for a dinner date. It's been frightening; all the
more so because the fink's data has been persuasive and seems to
have made complete financial sense to the two *Sunday Times*
experts. The next day I can't wait to confront them and ask:
'Well, what do you propose to do about the Jewish plot to dominate the world?' The journalists are very cool. 'The problem
is, if the company declares an overseas profit of £1 million
they don't have to say where it comes from. What we
have to do is prove there's been rigging of the Stock Exchange
and the only people who can do that are the Stock Exchange
Council who can ask to look at the records of the jobbers. And
they'll only do this if a company is folding or if the government
asks for an investigation. On the other hand,' the journalists
observe, 'don't you always do business with your friends? Who
else do you do it with? That's what business is about.'

The fink fascinates me and I make my own investigations,
sharing even more the excitement of being a journalist, 'naming
the guilty men'. I discover the fink worked for a large foreign
company as what they call a spare brain. He'd been with them
for ten years advising them on reorganisation and investments
while at the same time making a great deal of money from his
own speculations. He was finally sacked when it was discovered
he was making very long phone calls on the company's account
to far-away places in pursuit of those speculations. I pass this on
to the journalists. Weeks later the *Sunday Times* report on their
investigations into Mr A and conclude that everything seems to
be above-board.

THE BOOK OF THE PLAY 267

I understand why it's such an absorbing world, the business world, murky though it is. It's obvious the business section is prevented from reporting everything and I keep hearing about how Maxwell was unfortunate but that in fact, compared with some of the men and goings-on in the city, he was an amateur fallen angel. I learn, and must remember, to distinguish between industrialists, bankers and stockbrokers. The first consider themselves the real workers and mistrust city men as parasitical speculators. Though for their almost total indifference to human happiness, except in so far as it produces for them employees who are more manipulable, my fascination ends with wishing a plague on all their houses.

PART FOUR

'The system is awful. You can even make up the
quotes. It's like being in front of a firing squad.
Your victim can *ask* to see the copy but not
legally so.'

Censorship

I become interested in a reporter's article on the plight of low-
paid workers; he's excited to have discovered from government
sources that they will need pay rises of 42% a year if their
standard of living is not to fall. In his eagerness to attack 'thirteen
years of Tory misrule' his problem is to avoid his article becoming
too strident. How can he offer the facts and figures and be certain
their implications are understood? He confesses to operating an
in-built censorship and tones down the article; then, to his
pleasure, discovers he's underdone it. His seniors tell him not to
mess about, it's a shocking state of affairs and they want to say
so. The sentence; 'From this point on the only item which chips
away at increased earnings is income tax' is changed to the more
sharply worded: 'From this point on only income tax continues
to bite more deeply into increased earnings.'

The question of censorship inevitably emerges. There's a
difference of opinion. Someone says Lord Thomson doesn't
interfere: 'He's so scrupulous about the entire Times Newspaper
organisation that, despite owning 85% of the shares and Astors
only 15%, when he appointed an outside set of directors he
gave Astors an equal say on who those directors should be.'
Someone else cries: 'Nonsense! It's just this outside body that
exerts more pressure than anyone else. Whenever I'm interviewing X he never fails to remind me that he's a director of the
Sunday Times.' Another reporter tells the story of how: 'I once
had a phone call from Thomson to give me a story about the
struggle going on between Occidental Petroleum and another

company over drilling rights in the Persian Gulf. The head of Occidental is also a friend of Thomson and Thomson rang me up three times on the Saturday to make sure I was representing Occidental's story and urging that the British Government should come down on Occidental's side. Mind you, he wasn't urging me to write what I didn't want to — but what if he were?' Someone answers very sharply and firmly: 'Nothing would happen! Because *we* decide the journalism ourselves. We're not above taking any news tip from Lord Thomson; and we're not afraid to ignore one.'

I check that among the directors are: Sir Kenneth Keith of Hill Samuel — merchant bankers; Lord Shawcross, Chairman of the Takeover Panel; Sir Eric Roll, the economist and a director of the Bank of England; Sir George Pope, ex-manager of *The Times*; Sir Donald Anderson, ex-Chairman of P&O Shipping Lines; Lord Robens, ex-Chairman of the National Coal Board. 'Ah, ha!' I say, 'men outside the running of the newspaper but hardly outside the system.' 'That's the old conspiracy theory,' someone says. It's true, and as I don't hold it I'm embarrassed to be caught uttering it. I try to rebalance myself. 'But surely it's acknowledged that there are accepted means of them "letting it be known that ... "?' 'You have a concept of "them" and "us",' I'm told. 'Who's "them"? No person, no organisation can be monolithic. The idea that an administrative group of men can possibly share a single simple view of the world is nonsense.'

I didn't want to have to defend a conspiracy theory I didn't believe in; though I do believe that when the fundamental laws of competitive society are challenged then property, privilege and private enterprise, without needing to share a 'simple view of the world', close ranks. Not that a socialist can draw a complacent comfort from *that* simple analysis; the conflict is often confused in that the challengers (revolutionaries) seem so frequently to attract the worst demagogues, opportunists and fervourists of violence into their ranks that the poor 'people', in whose name all is done, are left with little but the two hells from which to choose. But I digress.

Someone rushed to defend the purity of the paper. 'I could tell you about every one of those Board members showing how we'd printed stories which went counter to the interests of the Thomson organisation. There was the time when we reported that the government in British Guyana had got in with the help of the C.I.A. — and at that moment a team of Thomson's men were there negotiating for the TV franchise which, of course they didn't get because they got blamed, wrongly, for the story. But *we* didn't hear a murmur from Thomson. Came back to us as a joke years later. Then there was the time there was talk of handing over a second TV channel to I.T.V., the original source of a lot of Lord Thomson's money. We opposed it! *Sunday Times* came right out against it! Not a murmur. And the time the colour magazine published some photographs of poor conditions for blacks in South Africa? The managing director of Thomson Organisation had his business facilities withdrawn but we heard not a single complaint from him. And what about that *Justice* report criticising the judiciary? Lord Shawcross wrote to *The Times* condemning us and he, don't forget, is a director, one of those men you mention as being "hardly outside the system". But we published and he made his protest in public. There are countless examples. No! If anything, we're perverse in the way we bend over backwards to maintain our purity. In fact we so want to demonstrate our impartiality we're often in danger of being unfair to those closest to us!'

I wander up to have coffee with my first day's guide, a pipe-smoking, sardonic man, and tackle him on the question of pressures from above: 'I suppose there does exist a kind of collective wisdom which might be biased in some kind of way because of confrontation with commercial influences.' He sucks on his pipe, thoughtfully, as though he's interested himself in his own observation. Then: 'No,' he changes his mind. 'That's a little naughty of me.' I pursue him: 'Look, I've never really believed in the conspiracy theory – the English capitalist system is too well established to need a conspiracy – but a newspaper like the *Sunday Times* must sometimes find itself confronted by a dilemma between its responsibility to print a story and a government warning about the consequences.' 'Mmm – yes – it does happen,' he talks like a landmine, unobtrusively; you don't believe such a peaceful, pipe-sucking landscape can explode; 'but on other papers, not this one. There are checks and balances you see, outside the system – the ecological balances of Whitehall, public opinion and the law; laws of privacy, of libel, of contempt. Like a fish in a pond, really. All you do is try to be a pretty good fish. Danger comes when fishes want to be birds.' There's no controlling a good explosion.

Ah well! Institutions, it seems, are like people – you must live with them on an intimate level in order to discover their truths. Journalism's pure and virgin daughter was the *Sunday Times* – if I really wanted to know her vices and virtues, if I really feared that journalism's lady of justice had lapses of honesty or succumbed to after-dinner seductions at the friendly tables of power then I should marry her myself and find out. But what journalist ever wedded *his* story – indeed it had been given me as an adage of journalism that if you became too involved with your subject you lost objectivity. Not that I accept the proposition of 'objectivity' – who but God?

I see Business News through to the end of the week. It's in this part of the paper where they ask me, with anxious good humour, if I'm preparing a report for the editor, and where I first heard the rumour that 'he's not writing a play at all but a series of articles for the *Observer*'. I tell everyone that I'm toying with the idea of writing a kind of insight on the *Sunday Times* but that it might be only for the internal amusement of the staff. Secretly I hope to produce an inspired piece which the editor can't resist or feels challenged to print. The wish to write a major piece of journalism has been nagging me for some time now — perhaps this will be it.

The last moments with Business News are touching. We go into the editor's office. 'Well,' he says, 'I think we've got a very good Business News tonight. That piece by —— , a great improvement, seems to get better each week, don't you think?' Soft glows of satisfaction appear, barely hidden by hearty remarks aimed at showing they didn't really hear the praise. The editor's in a good mood and distributes some of the praise in the direction of himself. 'We're the only ones who've really dared to go to town on the Spanish cholera epidemic.' And it's true, four columns seven inches high, plus a large map showing the cholera's movement. Very dramatic. But when I receive my own copy on the following morning the layout's changed. Why? Because on the Saturday they have read in an early edition of the *People* that Wilson is telling all about his financial state and his overdraft, and this important information is given place of honour at the top of the page while the editor's pride — the cholera spread — is cut; the map is gone and with it a column of copy. After the editor's bouquet-handing-out meeting I say to them: 'Well, that was sweet and comforting, no complaints from the ed.' 'Oh,' they say, brushing aside a need to acknowledge this, 'it's so depressing. The competition is so bad, so lazy. I mean, look at the *Observer* on I.P.C. They've asked no questions, done no homework, just looked at today's *Financial Times* and made a couple of phone calls. They've sent no one out to see anyone. It's so bad.'

'We're a bundle of news for a bundle of family.
Each section can be used by different parts of the
family. Doesn't matter if papa buys us for the
Business News as long as his wife is happy with the
review section and kids fight over the supplement.'

Foreign

Here is where I really feel at the centre of the world. The telex
tape ticks and pumps out the world's trials and tribulations; but
no one is satisfied they can do the job of reporting foreign news
adequately. 'It's too costly. We have a London office staff of
four and two secretaries plus the part-time services of the paper's
main feature writers; an overseas staff of five, plus a hundred
foreign correspondents of varying ability whom we share with
other papers and call "stringers".' I work out that it costs about
£257,000 to run the entire foreign wing for a year even though
they've got no full-time man in Latin America, Africa, Eastern
Europe, Moscow, the Far East or the Middle East. But a fascinating and perhaps more vivid reporting comes from un-
professional contacts who work in international business, political
or social organisations.

A phone call comes through from someone to say he's got a
trunkload of documents revealing the real truth about Biafra.
'Boy, just wait till you see what's inside this trunk, you've never
really seen a story like this one, boy this is really a big one.' They
sigh. 'If only he knew how sick we were of going through trunks
full of documents telling "the real truth" about Biafra. When
we asked shall we meet in his flat he said, "Oh no! Better be
somewhere where no one can see us". Trouble is you never know
about these people, although our experience is that it's usually the
man who rings up and says, "I don't suppose this will be of any
interest to you," who produces the most shattering documents.'

Here, more than in any other department of the newspaper, are to be found extraordinary pressures. Chance meetings with people who have been at the centre of world events can produce revelations of hair-raising horrendousness which, when certain powers get wind of them, produce threats to the life and family of the informant who is the one person who can finally sign to the truth of the information; and after months of investigation involving great expense and energy, the story has to be abandoned. 'Suddenly the sky is dark with flying lawyers.'

A pursuit of fact thoroughly supported by evidence inspires a less flippant tone in these offices than elsewhere. The observations of Business News that the Maxwell affair was insignificant compared to the other goings on in the city meet with stern rebuff here. 'I can't believe they really think that. Maxwell was an M.P. involved in deals worth nine millions — near to getting a cabinet post and bidding for two national newspapers, that's not insignificant.' I ask someone else (not from the Foreign department) whether Pergamon would have collapsed, with its attendant miseries for shareholders (about whom he seemed concerned), if they'd not done their investigation into the affair. 'Good question. We don't know. We *think* he'd have gone under even without our enquiries, but who knows?'

Is there feedback from their investigations? 'We're in the business of producing information rather than results; can't confuse the two or you end up with bad, emotional copy which weakens the credibility of the piece by its pleadings. There's only one issue which we've really gone to town on in order to produce results and that's Pakistan. The editor wants us to go on and on every week until something is done, even at the risk of becoming boring. And for a newspaper editor that's brave, don't you think?' Yes, I do think, but I want to know more, because if they don't produce results of some sort then they must surely be forced to look at the way they're conducting this 'business of producing information'. I'm told the story of an important Sunday journalist who became so involved in the Ulster crisis that she ended up organising and leading Catholic committees. I expressed great sympathy and admiration for such an action; it makes the journalist very human to have turned observation to commitment. Her stories will now have real insight and an honestly declared bias. '*If* she wrote stories. But now she can't. The two can't be mixed.'

An M.P. regarded five years ago as one of the bright young hopes in the Labour Party comes up as a topic of conversation. It's recalled that he'd held a junior minister's post from which he'd resigned. But though he's considered a friend by five members of the staff, yet they take time to remember which ministry it is and no one can remember what issue he'd resigned over.

'Poor bloke,' says one, 'he probably sweated over his decision for months and now no one remembers what it is.'

'Oh, I don't know. He probably thought he'd get his token resignation over and done with while he was still in only a junior post.'

'Still,' they muse, 'we don't remember. It's revealing.'

I'm asked if I've found out where the power lies in the newspaper. It's an innocent question which suddenly brings into focus the submerged patterns of fighting egos. I don't envy the Captain who has to control this team of brilliantly intimidating social terrorists.

A stranger comes in to try and persuade them that Agnew's impending visit to Greece is an important moment to write a story which gathers together and reveals the growing anti-junta pressures that exist. They listen carefully to his arguments: there's the pressure of the U.S. Congress to cut off arms supplies; rebellious parliaments in Bonn and Denmark - members of the North Atlantic Assembly, and even the American embassy in Athens is cold towards their Greek hosts. The foreign team are uncertain and pummel him with incisive questions.

'We don't *really* know how isolated Greece is, do we? Is U.S. support for them *really* collapsing? None of these things have actually happened. I mean we don't know and, with all respect, you don't know either.'

The stranger stands up to them well matching intelligence for intelligence.

'Only a minority of officers are behind the junta. If the majority had to choose between the Western Alliance and the junta they'd choose the Western Alliance.'

'Do we have anyone inside Greece who could produce concrete evidence to prove this?'

'We have contacts who can support the view but not provide the evidence.'

'Because you see, we get so many people telling us how this or that country's regime doesn't have the support of its peoples but little ever happens or looks as though it could happen.'

I can't resist asking them about the rumours that spies inhabit the Foreign department of the newspaper. What can they say? *They* wouldn't know. 'It's in the nature of something secret that it's kept secret.' Of course! But I enjoy the gentle blush that comes to their faces full of studious indifference. 'One thing is for certain, absolutely, the editor wouldn't hire anyone knowing he was employed by any secret service organisation.' It's an oddly naive thing to say. On the other hand they don't doubt that after a correspondent has been somewhere, or it's known he's going, they call him to lunch and ask him about his trip. 'But most journalists would tell them to fuck off or just have lunch and simply tell them what they'd just written in their articles.' What was suspected, however, was that certain overseas stringers who seemed to have acquired large houses and extraordinarily lavish interiors on mere journalists' salaries were also possibly used by intelligence agencies. But, much more likely, the rumour probably began because Ian Fleming was once foreign manager of the *Sunday Times*; or perhaps because everyone drew dark conclusions from the fact that Philby once wrote for the *Observer* and *The Economist*. Yer pays yer money and takes yer pick.

There are sad moments. A reporter has just struggled to knock his largest-ever story down from 4,000 to 2,500 words. With modest and expectant pride he asks one of his colleagues, a poker-faced heavyweight 'with an aggressive intelligence and great personal kindness': 'Well, what d'you think?' The piece is a frolicking account of the problems encountered in an assortment of Channel crossings. Our unsmiling heavyweight had responsibility for, and had himself succeeded in, pushing out space to accommodate someone else's account of the Libyan counter-coup. Bigger stuff, of course. Not your tender, minor witticisms about family travel, no! More important your cruelly damaging pontifications upon political thuggery. The lightweight waits for the heavyweight to comment. 'Reasonable, reasonable,' he says.

I at once beome interested in how the Libyan counter-coup is written. The Business News team have been sending it up.

'It's the classic Insight story, a parody of itself. "At 00.11 hours a B.O.A.C. Viscount Flight 0752 took off from Heathrow ..."'

Someone else picks up the story. '"At the same time a Russian Illyshin military trainer crashed inside Iraq territory killing all the Iraqui military passengers ..."'

'"Who can't sue of course and neither can the executed Sudanese coup officers .."'

'"Philby at that moment was eating his first hard-boiled egg in the Moscow restaurant ..."'

'"Four minutes, naturally ..."'

'"Meanwhile, the Prime Minister in Malta ..."'

'"At first sight all these far-flung incidents have no connection ..." And the awful thing is that the bloody story reads so well.'

It is, as was bitchily forecast, a predictable Insight piece: a detective-like assembly of facts reading in that low-tone American voice of mock instant drama — it's happening now, readers, as I write, this very moment. But the great political judgment at the end is rather like a schoolboy's triumphant ending to his studiously researched essay answering the question: 'The VC 10 was hijacked by Libya because Arab unity was at stake. Comment.' The article throws in a wide range of facts showing how hard the student has worked. 'The Libyan leader is an Arab visionary,' the article dramatically announces and then concludes, to my surprise, in the language of self-satisfied sixth-form scholarship: ' ... and that is why [dear teacher?] on Thursday morning he forced down the B.O.A.C. airliner to remove from it the two men who in his eyes were determined to undermine his personal vision of Arab unity by their secular challenge.' Yes, I think to myself, truly great stuff, and then I say — stop being bitchy, this particular heavyweight is one of the best minds on the paper. I'd just read his private memo to the committee on privacy — a responsible and cogently argued document in defence of the journalist's duty to investigate 'secret and well-protected misbehaviour' of a political or social — not private — kind.

But what can I do? I find myself thrown violently between respects and derisions for the journalist's manner; and it occurs to me that perhaps the people are better than their product. For example, after the brave fight put up for the retention of the female liberationist I, as well as thousands of others, look forward to her first article. And here she comes, out of the clouds, swooping down to make her first low-level attack on a product central to the cause of woman's liberation. Guess what? Vaginal deodorants! How imaginative of editorial to recognise such a talent. How courageous of the *Sunday Times*, so dependent upon advertising for its survival, to jeopardise potential revenue from advertising space bought by manufacturers of 'alternative female smells'. On the other hand, the record is impressive: Rachman, Cornfeld, Pergamon, Pakistan, Belfast. And weeks later, I read a finely argued piece of demolition called 'The Myth of the Silent Majority' which makes the simple point that the convenience of such a concept of silence is — the silence. If you say nothing then anybody can claim to speak for you. Such an article vindicates all journalism and if any debate opens on the strengths and weaknesses of the profession it could do worse than centre around the question why all journalism is not of such a level of writing.

'The essence of journalistic investigation is that it should usually concern matters which cannot be left to the police, or to other official bodies sometimes it may be the police or official bodies that should be investigated. There is perhaps no other country where the administration of society is carried out more honestly, humanely and conscientiously than in Britain. That does not mean that we have a society so perfect that we can afford to limit democratic scrutiny.'

Sports

Now, here is a proud and energetic section. Proud because 'until recently sports journalists were bottom on the rung of journalists, unless they were gentleman journalists. They were either simply fans, failed performers or bad writers on other parts of the paper. Today our aims are almost contrary — we would sooner produce better written than comprehensive copy.' Energetic for two reasons; the first being the obvious organisation needed throughout the week to despatch so many freelances over the country to cover the endless sporting events of this sporting isle. The second, more interesting; everyone is an 'expert' on sport. All sports departments suffer from the I'll-catch-you-game. Phone calls and letters are insistent and constant. Dealing in everyman's preoccupation I expect to encounter cockiness. Not so. 'Sports writers are always feeling guilty for not covering something more important, more useful. Classic example? The golf reporter covering golf in Ulster. What the hell was he doing covering golf in *Ulster*?'

My own attitudes to sport are ambivalent: disgust at the animal aggression of boxing mixed with admiration for its skill and physical endurance; fear of the hysterical football crowds mingled with a marvelling at their knowledge of the game; wonder at athletic feats alongside my personal boredom with even a minimal pursuit of bodily exercise. I decide to face the sports boys with what I believe is the safe side of my ambivalence. Thinking of my feeble muscles, stiff, complacent bones and loathsome little paunch I defend the healthy body/healthy mind approach. Their response shatters and diminishes. 'Sport is a fascist activity in that it's governed by rules against which there is no appeal and which, if applied to a democratic society, could not be upheld. What's more fascist than all that crap about a healthy body a healthy mind, and character being built on the playing fields of Eton? All balls. *What* character? That's the point.' That'll teach me to abandon my instincts and run with the hounds.

Still, I work out a defence for a relationship between an alert body and an alert mind. They give me no quarter. 'What great writer do you know ran a couple of miles before picking up a pen? A quarrel with his wife is more likely to stir him, a bit of private distress – that'll sharpen his emotions, not a handful of physical jerks.' Don't I know this is true, why am I arguing?

Yet I continue feebly about how fresh and prepared for anything one can be after a walk or a swim. 'If you're an idiot not even an Olympic medal changes that fact,' they reply. They've misunderstood, thank God! I tell them that I'm not suggesting a healthy body *made* a healthy mind but that given a lively mind to begin with it was enhanced by a fit body. They grudgingly concede the possibility.

I ask if different sports produce a different public. 'Rugby crowds are fair-minded and less violent because the violence is played out on the pitch. Wimbledon audiences tend to favour the underdog, love to see the leading player beaten. Some think there's violence in soccer crowds only when it's mirroring the violence of a particular game. Golf? All golfers are conservative and reactionary because the roots of their playing begin in the country clubs, crowds must be the same. But as soon as a sport is gambled over then the response of the crowd is uglier — boxing's a good example.' I remember later that I could have pointed to the pastoral quality of horse racing crowds.

My biggest delight is to have an old idea of my own confirmed. 'No sports centre should be built without arts facilities, and vice versa.' This idea is typical of their imaginative approach. 'We're not simply concerned with reporting sports events, we cover the sporting society also.' The narrow approach I'd expected is completely exploded. 'We'd even love to change over to the Arts Pages for six months.'

They give me a momentary guilt. 'Why have you left us till last?' It's not that they're resentful but feel it confirms their own view of themselves. 'We're the least important, I suppose?' I assure them it's partly the way it worked out and partly a reflection of my own ignorance of and scant interest in the subject — 'not a value judgment'. They don't seem convinced.

An industrial dispute occupies much of my days with them. The garage is being closed down because management want to rebuild on the site and economise on staff. Thirty-three men are to be made redundant. The messengers come out in sympathy and copy ceases to flow between departments. Articles are being written which may not be printed. It's a ghostly activity. Confusion exists about who is demanding what. The union says it doesn't want the decision withdrawn but only wants the date for closure postponed. Management say it's postponed the date once already. A document states that the compensation figure is £800. One of the garage men complains he's been told he won't get that sum. Rumour has it that the figure was a misprint. Everyone seems confused and helpless. The *Evening Standard* give the story to its front-page lead and for once, being on the inside, I can see that all they've done is quote from that internal document without making any attempt to get versions of the dispute from a direct confrontation with either management or union. Other journalists and various union representatives are lured to the Sports office whose editor is the chapel rep.

'*The difference between the production and the creative side is that we're prepared to work at all hours in order to get the paper out whereas production don't care a damn ... It's a question of whether they want to accept a situation in which 33 men are dismissed now with compensation and facilities for retraining, or whether 2,500 lose their jobs in a few years' time. I don't know why they can't see that. The man who can solve human relations problems like that is a genius ... Basically, as working-class men they don't care about the kind of journalism we produce, not that they've really studied it ... They've stopped the Securicor van from bringing in any cash so now the office girls can't be paid. Bloody-minded, isn't it? I mean they're only hurting their friends. Don't they know that most of us get paid monthly and the cheques go straight into the bank? ... It's this comprehensive system. The unions promise increased productivity* *for higher wages. What happens? The fun goes out of the job. The compositors used to follow through and care about — because they knew about — a sports story. They'd work right through the day. Now they're changed in the course of a day and editorial is faced with different compositors to whom they have to explain the layout all over again. They don't like it any more than we do ... It's not a normal working-class conflict. Those men drive Jaguars and own businesses on the side which their wives run for the two or three days they're here. They're just protecting their large salaries even at the expense of the rest of us. Do you know a cleaner here earns between £2,000 and £2,500 a year — the minimum salary for a journalist. Others on production can earn as much as £96 a week, more than the journalist's average wage.* They're working-class capitalists ... It's not true! All we're asking is that they withdraw the date of the 25th to give our branches time to discuss the situation. Now it's a matter of principle for us, and for management it's a question of personal pride that they've decided on that date and they don't want to shift from it. But we've got old men sitting down there who are terrified about what's going to happen in terms of pensions. No one's discussed pensions, pension arrangements are very unsatisfactory on this paper ... '*

A staff lawyer comes in to the middle of this sad confusion to ask what chances there are of them having a newspaper, he wants to know if he's going to be able to go to the races or not!

---

* Today's (1977) figures: a cleaner earns £3,650 for a 37½ hour week; minimum salary for a journalist is £4,500; a lino operator can gross £200 in a five-day week.

'You still here? You'd better write that play quickly
or you'll be writing about a defunct activity!'

Conclusions?

The journalist knows his world is among the least perfect of all
imperfect worlds. Most are raring to get out and write books –
the best of them do, frustrated by small canvases and the butterfly
life of their hard-earned thoughts and words. 'Conveyor belt
work, harsh, destructive, written in a hurry. I'm increasingly
irritated by the necessary approximations of journalism.' They
can't really be called callous just because they need the relief of
their own humour. 'Jesus! What a background I had! Were you
born in a ghetto? You were? Really? That's true? God, how I
resent my father for being so rich. All the best people were born
in a ghetto; look at Wesker, that's why he was born with a silver
typewriter in his mouth. If only my father had bought us a
ghetto, one we could go to for weekends, now that would have
been something!'

Yet, despite such disarming wit I can't rid myself of the
suspicion that they seem to *relish* the process of what they expose
more than they *care* about what is exposed. A very dubious
mechanism is at work when such a large number of people
assume for themselves the self-righteous responsibility of interfering to protect society against others whom *they* have decided
are interfering and self-righteous. Especially when their own
definition of their duty to investigate 'secret and well-protected
misbehaviour' is such a boomerang. Journalism may not be a
secret society but it is certainly one of the most 'well protected'.
Which editor would allow an investigatory profile of his newspaper to appear in his own columns? Certainly a gentleman's
agreement prevents them printing damaging information about
each other. The Sports department once printed two stories

about how the *Sun* manufactured a sports story. The editor of the *Sun* wrote to his counterpart on the *Sunday Times* and said 'Lay off'.

All motives, even for the serious journalist, are suspect except for his own. (I'm not referring to the anonymous little Farts of Fleet Street which every newspaper seems obliged to produce in gossip or comment columns all over the world.) And this makes him like the vicious prison officer whom society also justifies because he appears to be guarding society against its 'undesirables'. Yet, though someone must guard prisons, one is constantly tempted to wonder what kind of mentality opts for the job of ensuring men are deprived of their freedom. Similarly, though someone must guard society from charlatans, exploiters and political fraudulence, yet, one wonders, how carefully are those guards chosen for their wise ability to distinguish between honesty and dishonesty? How 'pure' can the soul be that traffics in human blemishes? And, further, are the pressures of journalism, profit-motivated as they must finally be, conducive to the exercise of perspicacious judgments? Like gladiatorial arenas, newspapers claim to know their audience's taste for blood. Hence little is celebrated, there is no conflict in that act; crucifixion is more dramatic. Although one famous columnist points out how journalism is a flat communicator: 'You can't see the face of the man writing the print. Television is much more alive. You can measure what's being said by the manner and face that's saying it. That's *real* conflict — vivid.'

But the soul, however insensitive, wearies of destruction; carnage must as well as 'love itself have rest'. An individual, an organisation, a society has a tone of voice, through it you can guess at its nature. What sort of nature lives in the arid, hollow tone of a hunter's horn behind which a smile leers? Society may wish to have its watchdogs, but continuous barking is a noise which, like the drip of the tap, can drive out all feeling with its bleak monotony; and sometimes innocent children are savaged.

But if we look at the difference between literature and journalism it becomes even more complicated. Fact may not be truth, and truth, if it has any chance of emerging, may rest in the need to interpret those facts, and both processes, the fictional and the journalistic, are human and thus imperfect; therefore I must concede as a playwright that art, like journalism, is presumptuous. But has journalism's infinitely smaller canvas the wrong kind of discipline to allow any but a superficial exploration of the complex subjects it chooses to handle? You feel you can argue with literature, temper its vicarious experience with your own. Journalism intimidates because its currency appears to be irrefutable fact and the great myth about himself and his profession to which the journalist succumbs is that he is engaged mainly in the communication of objective fact. But if we view journalism as a chemical compound and break it down we would find the ingredient 'fact' existed in only small quantities and even then lumbered by human impurities.

Journalism   = investigation or information or comment.
Investigation = 'facts' conveniently or maliciously leaked+(maybe) the evidence of documents—both selected and interpreted by journalists.
Information = selected 'facts'+ description, vivid or feeble depending upon individual powers of perception.
Comment   = personal opinions in leaders, reviews, features and gossip columns.

Yet even at the level of fact, which is not a discovery to be sneered at, the manner and amount of research done is questionable; the newspaper's library of old clippings is still the journalist's incestuous bed of primary knowledge; myths, prejudices, distortions and inaccuracies are perpetuated through his continual recourse to that brown-papered past of old copy. The cigarette packet warns that smoking can be a danger to health; no newspaper carries the warning, daily, that 'selective attention to data herein contained can be a danger to your view of the world'.

Still, someone who is not a journalist should be worried about writing a play with such a setting; it could end up contrived. And yet, there is a special part of the artist's experience which is not contrived: he or she has been the journalist's subject, frequently — as have been many public figures, and it is said of the sadist that only his victim truly understands him. In the end, the journalist, as recipient in a very special way of human experience, is the magnified personality in which drama deals. Though only engaged in handing on fragments of information he or she does so under the apparent omnipotence of daily print, which exaggerates his importance and tempts him to exaggerate pronouncements. The dilemma begins when he finds he can only inform without revealing, which leads him to simplify what is complex and confuse it for clarification; in the process he erodes ardours and enthusiasms, deflates egos so that not vanity but self-confidence cracks, and distorts our image of the world. His tragedy begins when each 'god' he self-righteously topples chips away at his own self-respect; the damage he does to others destroys a part of himself, and that's a very familiar state; no writer could find himself alien in that sad territory.

November 8th, 1971